A Poem at the Right Moment

Voices from Asia

1. *Of Women, Outcastes, Peasants, and Rebels: A Selection of Bengali Short Stories*. Translated and edited by Kalpana Bardhan
2. *Himalayan Voices: An Introduction to Modern Nepali Literature*. Translated and edited by Michael James Hutt
3. *Shoshaman: A Tale of Corporate Japan*. By Arai Shinya. Translated by Chieko Mulhern
4. *Rainbow*. By Mao Dun. Translated by Madeleine Zelin
5. *Encounter*. By Hahn Moo-Sook. Translated by Ok Young Kim Chang
6. *The Autobiography of Ōsugi Sakae*. By Ōsugi Sakae. Translated by Byron K. Marshall
7. *A River Called Titash*. By Adwaita Mallabarman. Translated and with an introduction by Kalpana Bardhan
8. *The Soil: A Portrait of Rural Life in Meiji Japan*. By Nagatsuka Takashi. Translated by Ann Waswo
9. *The Lioness in Bloom: Modern Thai Fiction about Women*. Translated, edited, and with an introduction by Susan Fulop Kepner
10. *A Poem at the Right Moment: Remembered Verses from Premodern South India*. Collected and translated by Velcheru Narayana Rao and David Shulman

A Poem at the Right Moment

Remembered Verses from Premodern South India

Collected and Translated by
Velcheru Narayana Rao
and David Shulman

UNIVERSITY OF CALIFORNIA PRESS

Berkeley *Los Angeles* *London*

University of California Press
Berkeley and Los Angeles, California

University of California Press, Ltd.
London, England

Library of Congress Cataloging-in-Publication Data

A poem at the right moment: remembered verses from premodern South India / collected and translated by Velcheru Narayana Rao and David Shulman.
p. cm.—(Voices from Asia; 10)
Includes bibliographical references.
ISBN 0-520-20847-1 (alk. paper).—ISBN 0-520-20849-8 (pbk.: alk paper)
1. Indic poetry—Translations into English. 2. Indic poetry (English). 3. India 18th century—Poetry. I. Nārāyaṇarāvu, Vēlcēru, 1932– . II. Series.
PK2978.E5P64 1997
891.4—dc21 96-29616
CIP

9 8 7 6 5 4 3 2 1

This book is dedicated to the memory of
Bommakanti Srinivasacharyulu
and
A. K. Ramanujan

saṃsāra-viṣa-vṛkṣasya dve phale amṛtôpame
kāvyâmṛta-rasâsvādaḥ saṅgatiḥ saj-janaiḥ saha

Contents

Preface

The following poems should not be on these pages. They should be sung, heard, swapped, quoted, commented upon, and enfolded in stories—all in an oral, spoken mode. These verses, which we refer to as *cāṭus*, are meant to be remembered and to be passed on by recitation. To reduce them to writing, in a collection contained between two covers, is to displace them from their living, collective context into a strangely silent medium. It is our hope and our experience that, despite this dislocation, their poetic charm and power somehow survive.

For their part, they insisted on being collected here. In the course of our work in various areas of south Indian literature, these poems and stories about the poets kept coming up, emerging naturally as we moved from text to text, from poet to poet. They were everywhere, binding these texts together, allowing them to resonate with and echo one another, providing living contexts. Moreover, taken as a whole, they offer a penetrating critical vision and understanding of the classical traditions of Telugu, Tamil, and Sanskrit. They reflect the internal perspectives of the communities in which these great literatures grew and flourished.

What began as individual encounters with verses and stories remembered and quoted to us eventually became a book. At first we exchanged *cāṭus* by daily e-mail, from Madison to Jerusalem and back. Later we set about more systematic commentary and translation. (This process also produced the headings we have given to each of the poems.) Although we present these verses individually, as one would encounter them in real life, our selection reflects our understanding of the *cāṭu* milieu as an interactive system, as we explain in the essay that follows the poems. We have chosen only such verses that we know to have been actively and collectively remembered, cited, and used; and in this respect this selection is the first of its kind in any language.

We relied mostly on our memories, but we would like to thank those individuals who remembered poems for us: Ashok Aklujkar, Padmanabh Jaini, J. Prabhakara Sastri, S. D. Lourdu, Bh. Krishnamurti, Arudra, and Muzaffar Alam. Wendy Doniger and Joyce B. Flueckiger responded warmly to verses that we sent to them as we were working. Lee Siegel and Stuart Blackburn offered helpful and appreciative comments. Sally Ketchum took on the thankless task of typing in diacritics in three languages. Our students in the seminar on Poetics and Metaphysics in Jerusalem in 1994–1995, and our colleagues at the Institute for Advanced Studies at the Hebrew University and at the Department of Literature, Ben-Gurion University, provided a foster community beautifully receptive to these newly displaced *cāṭus*. We wish to thank the John Simon Guggenheim Foundation for a fellowship to V. Narayana Rao in 1991, for work connected to these poets; the American Institute of Indian Studies, for a research fellowship in 1991–92; and the National Endowment for the Humanities, which generously supported our work in classical Telugu literature in 1994–96.

Note on Format

In the following pages, we usually begin with the translation of the *cāṭu* poem, followed by the original in Telugu, Tamil, or Sanskrit. (To identify which language is used, please refer to the index of English first lines.) Background information, contexts, and sources are noted at the bottom of the page. When no source is mentioned, the verse has been drawn from our memory. When a narrative is integral to the context, or to understanding the verse, we have presented it along with the poem. Such narratives are also part of the tradition as we know it, retold in our words.

Transliteration follows the *cāṭu* recitation forms and spelling, as distinct from the scholarly written spellings, throughout.

Introduction

1. WHAT IS A *CĀṬU*?

Where does a poem exist? What gives it life? Who is its author? How does it mean? Ask these questions, universal in relevance, in south India, and the answers may surprise you. We could couch these answers negatively, extrapolating from the late-medieval literary milieu, in order to highlight the contrast to our modern, print-oriented expectations. A poem does *not* exist within the pages of a book. It makes little sense to look for it there, or to read it silently. The poet to whom it may be ascribed is not its author. And as to meaning—a poem rarely means anything alone.

Stated positively: a poem, at least a good poem, exists in the memory or on the tongue of living connoisseurs. Its life consists in its oral recitation in some particular context, usually linked to a range of other contexts. Kālidāsa, the fourth-century Sanskrit poet living, let us imagine, in Ujjayinī, may or may not be the author of Kālidāsa's collected works, but he is certainly not the author of the living verses, in the above sense, associated with his name; these verses reproduce for us an image of the ideal poet, and they may evoke a tone or style. Meaning unfolds in the rich interplay of intertextual resonances, which position any given verse in relation to many others, to alternative and competing voices within an oral tradition, and to the ecology of themes and genres active within this mature literary culture. Within this culture, fixed "classical" texts, no doubt reproduced in writing, feed into the living world of oral citation and commentary; and this world also offers its own selection and presentation of such classical texts, in a distinct mode endowed with its own integrity. We thus distinguish between a recorded text—the fixed work in its entirety, in set sequence—and the received text, that is, the living work quoted, excerpted, sung, and selectively commented upon by the community that uses it. The recorded and received texts are never isomorphic, and it is the received text that fixes the author's voice and allows it to resonate in the continuing tradition.

Not all remembered, living verses claim authorship in this sense. Many are anonymous—creations of the oral medium, never even recorded graphically. Thousands of such verses are known, in Sanskrit, Telugu, Tamil, and other south Indian languages.[1] Together, they make up the deep and ramified system of literary creativity in each of these languages—a system which crystallized, we believe, in medieval times, but which must have

1. Telugu is the language of Andhra Pradesh, and Tamil the language of Tamil Nadu, both states of southern India. Other major languages of this region are Kannada and Malayalam. Sanskrit, the ancient language of India, a "father-tongue," was used creatively alongside these mother-tongues throughout medieval and premodern times.

drawn on much earlier forms of oral transmission and commentary. The verses that make up this system are known as *cāṭu* ("charming utterance") in Telugu and Sanskrit, or *taṉippāṭal* ("single stanza") in Tamil.

Here is an example:

annāti gūḍa haruḍavu.
annātini gūḍakunnan asura-guruṇḍ'auḍ'-
anna tirumalarāya
kann' ŏkkaṭi ledu gāni kantuḍave le

When you are with a woman
you are God himself with all three eyes.
Without her, you are just like Śukra, teacher of the antigods.
Brother Tirumalarāya—you're as handsome as the Love God
minus one eye.

This poem is about a king who is blind in one eye. Attributed to the clown-poet Tĕnāli Rāmaliṅgaḍu (Tĕnāli Rāma), it is said to have been composed after a series of hackneyed, hyperbolic eulogies had been recited. The poet uses the well-known mythological images of Śiva, who has three eyes, and Śukra, teacher of the demons, who is blind in one eye. Although seeming to praise the patron, the poem still retains a critical edge, as it exposes the patron's deformed face to public view. Is this praise or ridicule? Or is the poet ridiculing other poets who heap praise on the patron? All these possibilities are present, dependent on context and tone. Indeed, herein lies the value of verses like this, which retain their charm far beyond the actual context of their composition and long after the time of their authors. They are recited for pleasure, applied to new contexts, or used to recreate imagined older contexts. Such verses are remembered by the hundreds. They circulate in oral tradition, an oral tradition of a literate people.

In premodern south India, one pastime for literate people was to recite such *cāṭu* verses from memory, usually in small groups. Everyone knew them; and if ever these educated listeners came across a particular verse that was new, or existed in a different version, they would immediately memorize it and make it part of their repertoire.

Such verses are attributed to a number of authors, from the "classical" Kālidāsa (in Sanskrit), Śrīnātha (in Telugu), and Kampaṉ (in Tamil) to recent poets only locally known. Aesthete-kings, libertine-poets, ministers, scholars, soldiers, holy men, not so holy but ravishingly beautiful women—all these parade through these verses. Most poems have a story that goes with them, and each is invariably memorable, a perfectly worked-out expression of skilled composition, though often disarmingly simple. These *cāṭus* have appealed to, and shaped, the taste of generations of people. Together they represent a literary culture and a tradition built up over centuries. They bring to mind, in addition to aesthetic judgment, a host of literary, political, and cultural contexts, indeed, a whole world view.

Modern literary historians have struggled to identify the "historicity" of the poets, their patrons, and the legends that are associated with these verses. It has been common for historians of literature to relate the legends along with the *cāṭu* verses and then dismiss them as historically unreliable, while still trying to reconcile the names that occur in these legends with historically identifiable persons, thus using them to construct a chronology of poets. Historians regret the fantastic nature of the legends, but they find them turning up everywhere, even in inscriptions or family or local "histories" (*praśastis* and *vaṃśāvalis*). Irresistible as they are, these *cāṭu* verses and the legends that go with them have compelled the attention of scholars such as C. P. Brown, the nineteenth-century administrator-savant who wrote:

> These verses I collected on account of their beauty, the celebrity of the composers, or their utility in illustrating the language. Many, both ancient and modern, may be found that have been preserved by oral tradition alone. I propose to arrange them in books containing four or five hundred in each.[2]

Following Brown, Telugu pandits published anthologies of *cāṭus*. Influenced by the new styles of scholarship introduced by Western education, they sought to preserve these verses as literary curiosities. Later scholars like Veṭūri Prabhākara Śāstri (in Telugu) and M. Raghava Aiyangar (in Tamil) have, in turn, produced well-edited anthologies of *cāṭu* verses. Using these anthologies as sources, other scholars extended the historical and chronological investigations further to produce a history of the development of the *cāṭu*. The *cāṭu* anthologies offer a recorded corpus of the most prominent verses, though this corpus is no more than a pale reproduction of the lively oral tradition. In keeping with the Victorian morality of the times, early editors of these anthologies took care to censor the obscene verses and tried to protect the reputation of great poets like Śrīnātha, to whom many such verses were attributed, by rejecting such attributions or by cleaning up the text. In situations where this could not be done within the standards of modern text editing,

2. C. P. Brown, D 2884, cited in Bŏmmakaṇṭi Śrīnivāsâcāryulu and Bālantrapu Nalinīkāntarāvu, *Tĕlugu cāṭuvu: puṭṭu-pūrvôttarālu* (Madras: Kaḷyāṇi Pracuraṇalu, 1983), 7.

the objectionable parts of the verse were often deleted, replaced by dots.

Both Brown and his south Indian followers confused two distinct meanings of the term *cāṭu*—one that was recorded in books on literary theory, and the other known only in popular usage. *Cāṭu* in the *alaṃkāra* literary-theoretical works meant an unconnected stanza, sometimes put together in clusters of five, six, seven, or more. A single *cāṭu* verse of this type is called *muktaka*, "a separate stanza" (again, *taṉippāṭal* in Tamil),[3] and there are fourteen varieties of *cāṭu* clusters. The *alaṃkāra* theoreticians thus recognize *cāṭu* as a free-standing stanza or a cluster of stanzas unconnected to a narrative sequence. There are many such *cāṭus*, which were composed as independent verses, and which thus fall naturally into the category recognized by the poeticians; and there are many more that are anthologized as independent verses, often lifted out of context from a longer narrative poem. These poems have acquired the status of *muktaka-cāṭus* by being used as such. There are anthologies of such *cāṭus* in Telugu from the fifteenth century onward (beginning with Maḍiki Siṅganna's *Sakala-nīti-sammatamu*).

In contrast to the above, a *cāṭu* in popular usage is a *remembered* poem, used in social communication, circulated orally. Whether it is a written poem in oral circulation or a verse composed orally is an issue of little significance in the oral-literary culture of premodern India. What is important is that a *cāṭu* is remembered and used in social communication among a com-

3. On the Tamil *taṉippāṭal*, including major collections, see K. V. Zvelebil, *Tamil Literature* (Wiesbaden: Otto Harrassowitz, 1974), 7, 51–54. Thus Tamil, too, conflates the two kinds of *cāṭu* in a single term.

munity of people who constitute themselves as a group by sharing a certain body of knowledge and ideology. The *cāṭu* defines, expresses, and communicates such knowledge and ideology among specific communities.

Thus, two criteria determine a *cāṭu* of this type: it must be remembered, known by heart, available for oral recall; and it must be employed in social communication. In this sense, a *cāṭu* is not really an isolated verse, even if it appears as such. It is an integral part of a system of communicated and shared knowledge, often with strong intertextual connections and interactive relationships between these apparently independent verses. We are looking at a well-defined body of verses, many with associated stories and contexts, that has maintained itself as a coherent whole through oral communication from generation to generation among a specific group of people (more precisely defined in the After-Essay). In this sense this corpus constitutes a tradition. Common knowledge of these verses constitutes a literary community not necessarily composed of experts and specialists at home in the royal courts or other such exclusive establishments. These people were literate, which is not to say merely that they could read and write but to suggest an analytical linguistic competence and an awareness of "grammar" in the widest sense (including phonology, metrics, and poetics)—an educated awareness which could, incidentally, be largely transmitted by oral instruction.[4] Indeed, the primary mode of communication among this community was always oral. As such, it

4. On oral literacy of this type, see V. Narayana Rao, "Purāṇa as Brahminic Ideology," in *Purāṇa Perennis*, ed. Wendy Doniger (Albany: State University of New York Press, 1993), 85–100.

always privileged the metrically composed verse, memorable and memorized, as the chief medium of communication. These verses circulated in what we might call a premodern cultural public space, somewhat similar to the public space of the European bourgeoisie, as defined by Habermas.[5] In fact, the shared *cāṭu* verses, circulating everywhere in more or less the same form, actually *created* a public space for literary and cultural discussion.

Unfortunately, this popular concept of *cāṭu*, which has been familiar for centuries in south India, has escaped the attention of practically every scholar who worked on *cāṭus*.[6] Conceptually dependent on written texts, both Sanskritic and Western, scholarship lost sight of prevalent usage, though it was known to the scholars from their own experience. Collections of *cāṭus* have been assiduously but indiscriminately made, including every verse which could possibly be considered independent, every oral or extempore poem, and every legend and story associated with such verses. Defining a *cāṭu* and identifying its actual author have become favorite scholarly pastimes. Thus it may be argued, for example, in the factual mode, that a particular *cāṭu* attributed to Śrīnātha was not actually his—for it is too obscene to have been composed by such a cultured poet. The fact that a *cāṭu* is a creation of the community, and that each such verse is an integral part of a community repertoire, has been over-

5. Jürgen Habermas, *The Structural Transformation of the Public Sphere: An Inquiry into a Category of Bourgeois Society* (Cambridge, Mass.: MIT Press, 1991).

6. A notable exception is Bŏmmakaṇṭi Śrīnivāsâcāryulu in *Tĕlugu cāṭuvu*, 15.

looked. Part of the reason for this is that such communities are themselves rapidly disintegrating with the emergence of new towns and cities—even though one can still find today, after two centuries of attrition, living communities of people who swap these verses for pleasure. More significantly, Western modes of learning and Western styles of patronage introduced a new sense of chronology, textual authority, and historicity into traditional literary scholarship. New questions were asked. When was Śrīnātha born, and how long did he live? How could a poet curse a king out of his empire simply by composing a verse against him? How do two poets who belong to two different centuries, to say nothing of poets who never existed anywhere at any time, meet and exchange verses? Most devastating of all, how could great poets compose these disgustingly erotic, pornographic verses? Traditional south Indian culture began to be both defensive and imitative. Scholars of literature became historians examining inscriptions or editors working on critical editions. A new native elite emerged, educated in Shakespeare and Milton, Wordsworth and Keats, while the old scholarship was fighting for survival. *Cāṭu* verses were irritating for the new scholarship, which dismissed them as figments of imagination belonging to a people who have no sense of history or chronology. Still the verses persisted, too compelling to be overlooked, too beautiful to dismiss.

Oral circulation, in the absence of a written text with an author's name, has relegated the *cāṭu* to the periphery of literature as studied today. Even more unfortunate, the commitment to chronological literary history has disturbed the very notion that there was a living tradition of *cāṭu* usage, which generated and maintained a whole culture. Before the advent of linear history and personal biography, printed books, and the Western concepts of authorship, texts, and authenticity, the *cāṭu* tradition represented the very center of literary life. It reflected the main concepts basic to literary understanding and appreciation—concepts of poet, text, and style, of what constitutes a good poem, and judgments about the relative status of texts and their authors. It is here that the great battles of literary criticism were fought and that the public vision of poets and their position was recorded. Written texts are flat and silent; it is their use that gives them the heights and depths, the contours of life. Unrecorded in writing, the *cāṭu* tradition provided the ideal space in which to register community acceptance and appreciation.

Indeed, one might argue that oral communication insures acceptance by the community more than written communication does. The fact that a verse or tale is recited or retold, over and over again, for generations is a greater and more dependable indication of such acceptance than statistics of sold copies or press reviews. The very fact that a book is written does not, in itself, indicate the number of people that read it—or, still less, the number of people who like it. Even in the days of publishing houses with recognized status, press runs, best-seller lists, reviews, and publicity strategies, there is no guarantee that a book which sells well is also read and appreciated by all those who purchase it. As with Robert Lynd's pharmacists, who make money from medicines people forget to take, we might say publishers make money from books people neglect to read. Like economists who need the velocity of circulation to determine the quantity of money, we need to know the velocity of circulation of books to understand their impact on society. A million dollars kept in a vault, out of circulation, do zero work as money; a book well written but not read has zero influence on the community. One sure way of finding the velocity of circulation of books in premodern south India is to look into the *cāṭus*. If a poet does not have a *cāṭu* about him, or by him, in popular use, we may safely assume he is not a well-known poet.

2. WHO IS A POET?

The *cāṭu* tradition did more than record the popularity and critical acceptability of a poet in the eyes of a literate community. It also defined the very idea of a poet as understood by this community. Here a poet is supposed to personify the powerful voice given to him by the goddess of speech herself, or by some such superior deity. A poet is not one who has merely learnt the skill of making verses; he or she has the power to make reality conform to his or her speech. Poets' "biographies," in the *cāṭu* world, always demonstrate this power. Let us take the well-known example of Bhīmakavi, a "curse-poet" located by the Telugu tradition at a very early point in its evolution.

> Bhīmakavi's mother was a widow living at her parents' home. One day she went with a group of pilgrims to the Śivarātri festival at Dakṣârāma, the temple to Bhīmeśvara-Śiva. She saw her fellow pilgrims praying to the god for boons. Skeptical herself, she said to him: "If you give me a son like you, I will give you a tank of water as oil for your lamps and four tons of sand for your food." The god was pleased at this challenge and visited the widow that night; he slept with her and promised her a son, whom she was instructed to name after him.

She called the boy who was born Bhīma. One day his playmates mocked him for being a bastard. He ran to his mother and threatened to hit her with a rock if she didn't reveal the name of his father. She said: "That rock in the temple is your father; go ask him." Now the boy went into the temple and threatened to hit the god with a rock. Bhīmeśvara-Śiva, afraid, appeared before him in his true form and announced that he was, indeed, the boy's father. "In that case," said the boy, "from now on whatever I say must come true." The god granted him that boon.

One day there was a Brahmin feast in the village, held behind locked doors; Bhīmakavi was not invited. He cursed the Brahmins in the following verse:

gŏppalu cĕppukŏñcu nanu k̲ūṭik̲i paṅk̲tik̲i rāk̲u mañcu ī
trippuḍu bāpal' andarunu tiṭṭiri k̲āvunan ŏk̲k̲amāru ī
appamul' anni k̲appalâyi annamu sunnamugāga mārucun
pappunu śāk̲amul pulusu paccaḍulun ciru rālu k̲āvutan

Full of their own greatness, these lousy Brahmins
insulted me and threw me out of their feast.
I'll turn their fried cakes into frogs,
their rice into lice, and all the side dishes
into fishes.

When the Brahmins, witnessing these transformations, begged his forgiveness, Bhīmakavi sang a second verse:

ghanuḍau vemulavāḍa vaṃśajuḍu dak̲ṣârāma bhīmeśa nan-
danuḍ' ī bhīmanay añcu gurt'ĕrigi nindal māni nan gauravam-
bunan ī viprulu cūcir' anduvalanan pūrvasthitin jĕndi bho-
jana-vastu-prak̲arambul' anniyu yathâsvasthambul' au gāvutan

I'm Bhīmanna, son of Lord Bhīma himself,
born into the great Vemulavāḍa clan.

Now these Brahmins know me, and look at me with respect.
I take back my curse: let their food
become food.[7]

Bhīmakavi, famed in the *cāṭu* tradition as *śāpânugraha-samartha*, "capable of cursing and blessing," is said to have cursed kings and destroyed and restored thrones. He also made trees dry up and dry wood sprout. The word of the *cāṭu* poet is never empty of effect; it changes, or indeed creates, a reality in conformity with the vision implicit in the poet's speech. Note, in this sense, the importance of the seemingly tautological statement at the end of the second verse; food becomes food. Indeed, any thing or being becomes itself only through the mediation of the poet's charged words. We will return to this theme in the After-Essay in connection with the metaphysics of language implicit in the *cāṭu* tradition.

Such images of the poet have a venerable antiquity in southern India. Already the Caṅkam poems show us poets embroiled in complex, sometimes antagonistic, relations with their patrons, to the point where the poet may curse a recalcitrant lord—always to immediate, concrete effect.[8] There is a striking continuity from these ancient contexts to the medieval *cāṭu* world, where the poet controls language and, therefore, reality itself. Often this control is revealed as superior even to the power of a

7. See Gurajāḍa Śrīrāmamūrti, *Kavi-jīvitamulu*, 5th ed. (Madras: Vāviḷḷa Rāmasvāmiśāstrulu and Sons, 1955), 1–5.

8. See discussion and examples in D. Shulman, "Poets and Patrons in Tamil Literature and Literary Legend," in *The Powers of Art: Patronage in Indian Culture*, ed. Barbara Stoler Miller (Delhi: Oxford University Press, 1992), 89–119; also V. Narayana Rao, "Kings, Gods, and Poets: Ideologies of Patronage in Medieval Andhra," 142–59, in the same volume.

god, whom the poet does not hesitate to ridicule. Take the case of Kāḷamekappulavar (Kāḷamekar), perhaps the paradigm of the *cāṭu* poet in Tamil. Like Bhīmakavi, Kāḷamekar received the gift of poetry from a divine source.

> Born a Vaiṣṇava in Śrīraṅgam, this temple Brahmin had "converted" to Śaivism because of his love for a dancing girl at the nearby Śiva shrine of Tiruvāṉaikkā. One night he fell asleep in a hallway in the temple precincts and was locked in. Another devotee was also there, absorbed in meditation on the goddess; but when she appeared before him in the guise of a young girl, chewing betel, and offered to feed him some of the betel from her mouth, he chased her away in disgust. (This is the standard human failure to recognize the god or goddess when he or she comes closest.) So the goddess woke up the sleeping Kāḷamekar instead; his mouth automatically popped open, and she slipped in the betel. At once he began to sing, improvising sweet Tamil verses with the full, driving force of a dark monsoon-cloud (*kāla-megha*). In this guise he traveled through south India, engaging in poetry contests at various small courts. At Tirumalairāyaṉpaṭṭaṇam he defeated a host of minor poets, led by one called "Over-Sweet" (Atimaturakavi = Skt. Atimadhurakavi), in a dramatic contest of improvisation, in which Kāḷamekar was suspended in an iron cage over a blazing fire. A single mistake in meter, grammar, or meaning would have resulted in immediate death. Despite his victory, however, the local lord refused to honor the poet, so the latter cursed Tirumalairāyaṉpaṭṭaṇam to be swallowed up by dust. It has been buried ever since.[9]

9. U. Ve. Cāminātaiyar, *Niṉaivu-mañcari* 2 (Madras: Kalaimakaḷ, 1953), 58–60.

One day Kāḷamekar's arch-rival, Atimaturakavi, visited Śiva's temple in Tiruvārūr and began a verse on the god in his role as destroyer of the demons' Triple City:

nāṇ ĕṉṟāl nañc' irukkum naṟ-cāpam kaṟ-cāpam
pāṇan tān—

A bowstring sinister as poison.
A bow hard as rock.
As for the arrow—

This, unfortunately, was as far as Atimaturakavi could go; he wrote these words on the temple wall and went away. The references were clear enough: when Śiva went to war against the Triple City, he took Mount Meru as his bow and the serpent Vāsuki as the bowstring. Viṣṇu, the god who swallows up the earth at the time of cosmic destruction, became the arrow—but Atimaturakavi was unable to complete this element of the mythic scene. Kāḷamekar, however, happened by and saw the truncated verse written on the temple wall; at once he completed it in the mode of *nindā-stuti*, "praising the god through blame":

—maṇ tiṉṟa pāṇame tāṇuve
cīr ārūr mevum civaṉe nīy ĕppaṭiyo
nerār puram ĕritta ner

—the arrow bites the dust.[10]
And you yourself are a stone pillar,
God in Ārūr:
with weapons like these, how could you ever
win a war?

10. The reference is to Viṣṇu's act of swallowing the earth as well as to the child Kṛṣṇa's fondness for eating dirt (see example at the end of the After-Essay).

Kāḷamekar wrote these concluding lines on the temple wall and went away. When Atimaturakavi returned to Tiruvārūr and read the completed poem, he at last recognized Kāḷamekar's great gift.

But it was too late. Soon after, the great poet died, and his erstwhile rival could do no more than compose the following lament over his funeral pyre, quoting Kāḷamekar himself (from the verse the two had composed together):

ācu kaviyāl akilav ulak' ĕṅkum
vīcu pukaḻ kāla-mekame pūcurā
viṇ kŏṇṭa cĕn talaḻil vekutey aiyaiyo
maṇ tiṉṟa pāṇam ĕṉṟa vāy.

You rained down poems on the whole world
like a dark monsoon-cloud,
but red flames leaping toward heaven
burn the lips that once sang
of an arrow
that bites the dust.[11]

Kāḷamekappulavar's story shows us many of the standard features of the *cāṭu* poet: the divine source of his gift (in essence, an *unconscious* facility with language); the existential position of poetry, improvised by the poet who is literally suspended between life and death; the poet's ability to transform reality, to bless or to destroy; the intense rivalry that nearly always exists between the poets recognized by the tradition, and that some-

11. Text in *Kāḷamekam taṉippāṭalkaḷ*, ed. Puliyūrk Kecikaṉ (Madras: Mullai nilaiyam, 1993), 22–23. We have preferred the text of the second verse as it appears in *Taṉippāṭaṟ-ṟiraṭṭu*, ed. M. Vīraveṟ Piḷḷai (Madras: P. Na. Citampara Mutaliyār Brothers, 1940), 1:271 (where the Twin Poets, Iraṭṭaiyar, replace Atimaturakavi).

times expresses a conflict or categorical division between different kinds of poetic creativity, or between styles; and the pathos nearly always evident at the poet's death, which produces a rich genre of *cāṭu* laments. We also call attention to the major theme, to which we will return, of verses begun by one poet and completed by another (we will call these *para-pūrita* verses, "finished by another"); in the present case, the superior poet is the one who dares to finish a verse that pokes fun at God himself.

There is yet another important feature of the medieval *cāṭu* poet: he or she is naturally omniscient. "The poet can see what even the Sun cannot see" (*ravi gāñcani co kavi gāñcune gadā*). This theme recurs regularly in the *cāṭu* traditions about Kālidāsa, the greatest of Sanskrit poets. His story, in the *cāṭu* perspective, begins with the familiar motif of poetry as a divine gift.

> At first Kālidāsa was an illiterate shepherd. The minister of the local king swore revenge against his king because the latter refused to give his daughter to the minister's son; so the minister tricked the king into giving his daughter to the most foolish man he could find—the lout Kālidāsa. On the nuptial night, when the princess discovered that she had been deceived, she instructed Kālidāsa to go into Kālī's temple during the night and close the doors from inside; the goddess would come back in the early hours of the morning after her rounds in the city and would want to reenter her temple before dawn, before anybody in the city could see her. Kālidāsa—this was his bride's plan—should refuse to open the doors for the goddess unless she gave him learning, or *vidyā*. Kālidāsa followed these instructions exactly: Kālī was distressed when she found herself locked out of her temple; Kālidāsa insisted that he be given *vidyā* as a condition for opening the door. The goddess threatened him,

but he was adamant. At last Kālī gave in and asked Kālidāsa to open the door a crack and stick out his tongue. She then inscribed the seed-syllables, *bījâkṣaras*, on his tongue.[12] Instantly, Kālidāsa broke into a highly erudite poem about Kālī, and from that moment on, he was a poet.

As such, he was also gifted with the poet's vision, an all-embracing, precise and detailed omniscience. Many stories illustrate Kālidāsa's gift: for a typical example, see page 82. The same faculty applies to the outstanding figures of the Tamil and Telugu traditions. In Tamil, it is primarily Kampaṉ, the author of the Tamil version of the *Rāmāyaṇa*, who is elevated to this status (and, like Kālidāsa, associated with the goddess Kālī).[13]

One night the Chola king was prowling the streets of his city (as Tamil kings, curious and anxious, tend to do at night), when he came upon the temple of the gruesome goddess Kālī—presumably on the outskirts of the town, where Kālī usually lives. Peering through the door, he saw the demon-servants of the goddess busy grating sandalwood on stone, to make the cooling sandal paste with which she is adorned. (Kālī is a hot and terrifying goddess, always in need of cooling.) Somehow, by chance or forgetfulness, or perhaps in impudent self-confidence, one of these demons fingered the paste that was meant for the goddess, even lifting it to his nose to smell its strong fragrance. A fellow demon, working beside him, warned him not to do this, but it

12. Compare the Aridharma story in A. L. Becker, "Aridharma: Framing an Old Javanese Tale," in *Writing on the Tongue*, ed. A. L. Becker (Ann Arbor: Center for South and Southeast Asian Studies, University of Michigan, 1989), 281–320.

13. The historical Kampaṉ probably lived in the twelfth century, in the Choḻa period.

was too late—there was no way for him to hide the subtle fragrance that adhered to his fingers. What else could the companion do, intent on safeguarding the rights of the goddess, except to cut off the offending hand?

All this the king witnessed, and he was amazed. He went straight to Kampaṉ's house and knocked on his door. First to answer was the poet's son, Ampikāpati, a poet in his own right. Sleepily—for the king had woken him—he sang the first half of a Tamil poem:

karaikku vaṭakk'irukkum kāḷikkāḷ ammaikk'
araittu vaḻicantai tŏṭṭ' appey—

In Kālī's temple, on the northern shore,
they were grinding sandalwood on stone
to a fine paste. A ghoul
touched it—

This was as far as Ampikāpati could go—a precise but rather prosaic account of what the king had seen. At this point Kampaṉ, poet and father, awoke and groggily sang the final two lines, as if describing his own dream:

uraittum
maṟaikkav ariyātavaṉpeyin kaiyaik
kuṟaikkumāṉ kūrkatti kŏṇṭu

though he had been warned.
They cut off his hand: there was no
escaping. Could anyone hide
such fragrance?

Neither of the two poets had to witness the event in order to know it, and to embody it in a poem—though it is the great poet Kampaṉ, alone, who can complete the verse.[14] A lesser poet may begin, but the omniscient master has to finish. Like so many *cāṭus*, this one also carries a suggestion of metapoetic commentary: the father's first word, filling the empty gap where his son has become stuck, puns on two homophonous roots, *urai* (both "to speak" and "to scrape [sandalwood]"); poetry itself, the verse seems to hint, carries the dangers, the promise, the potential break or cut, and the enduring, unmistakable fragrance of the sandal paste offered to the goddess.

A very popular and persistent legend about Kṛṣṇadevarāya—historically, the emperor of the Vijayanagara super-state at Hampi (1509–29), but in the *cāṭu* world, a synoptic image of the ultimate king and patron—says that he had in his court eight great poets, *aṣṭa-dig-gajas*, seated in eight different directions like the eight cardinal elephants that bear the burden of the earth. One of these poets was Mukku Timmana, who was given as a wedding present (*araṇapu-kavi*) from the family of Cinnādevi, the king's beloved wife. One morning when Kṛṣṇadevarāya was about to leave for his court, he caught sight of the lovely Cinnādevi as she was drying her hair after her bath. The king was moved to kiss her, parting her hair and pulling off her sari. Shyly, she tried to cover herself with her hand—thereby only increasing the king's desire. When he arrived at the court, he proposed the following line as a riddle (*samasyā*) to be completed by his poets:

vi/sphurita-phaṇā-maṇi-dyutula pŏlp'agu nāga-kumāruḍoy anan

14. For a longer discussion of this stanza, see D. Shulman, "Dreaming the Self in South India," in *Dream Cultures: Toward a Comparative History of Dreaming*, ed. G. Stroumsa and D. Shulman, in press.

as a Cobra-Prince might spread
his great gem-encrusted hood
to guard a hidden trove.[15]

Mukku Timmana immediately completed the verse by composing the first three lines to go with the king's last line:

varuḍu cĕraṅgu paṭṭinanu valv' aṭu vīḍina ḳānta siggucen
urutara-ratna-dīdhitulan ŏppĕḍu ḍāpaliḳela mūyagā
ḳaram' amarĕn ḳaramb' apuḍu ḳāma-nidhānamu gāciyunna—

When the lover pulled at her sari
and it came loose,
in sudden shyness she moved to hide
her treasure-house of love
with her left hand, luminous
with vivid stones—

[as a Cobra-Prince might spread
his great gem-encrusted hood
to guard a hidden trove.]

The poet was perfectly aware of the bedroom scene without having been there to witness it. He expresses his visionary knowledge by converting a particular incident into a delicate love poem, built deftly around the crafted metaphor that he was given as a starter. Note that no names are mentioned in the poem: anyone can now identify with the two lovers. This is the true measure of the poet's achievement. A nuanced reading of the poem also reveals an important distinction between its structure and that of other such instances of the poet's omni-

15. Folk belief tells us that the cobra extends his hood to protect the treasures he has amassed.

science. When Kālidāsa is offered a half-line by Bhoja, there is an expectation, it seems, that the poet will complete the line because he already knows what happened, as is the case with Kampaṉ and Ampikāpati in the story just cited. In the case of Timmana, however, the power of the completed verse lies in the aesthetic absorption of the initially given image—in itself open-ended, capable of being used in various ways—by the generalizing and gently eroticizing lyricism of the first three lines. What began as a private incident between two specific persons, not meant to be publicized, has ended up as a complex love lyric, now majestically sealed by the final line.

Another of Kṛṣṇadevarāya's poets was Dhūrjaṭi, famed for the supernal sweetness of his verses. One day the King wondered why Dhūrjaṭi's verses had this quality, and he presented this problem as a puzzle for the other poets:

stutamatiyainay āndhrakavi dhūrjaṭi palkulak' ela galgĕn īy-
atulita-mādhurī-mahima—

Why do Dhūrjaṭi's Telugu poems
overflow with sweetness incomparable?—

To which, the court jester Tĕnāli Rāmaliṅgaḍu replied:

—hā tĕlisĕn bhuvanâikamohanôd-
dhata-sukumāra-vāra-vanitā-janatā-ghanatâpahāri-
santata-madhurâdharôdita-sudhā-madhu-dhārala groluṭañ jumī

I know why. It comes from constant drinking,
to quench his constant pain,
at the honeyed lips of wild young courtesans
who drive the world insane.

Once again, the poet—in this case the subversive jester—knows *a priori* the real cause and meaning of a given theme. Note how he also manages to concretize and literalize the issue, at the same time translating the classical quality of "sweetness" (*mādhurya*), recognized by the poeticians and theorists, into another, entirely embodied mode.

It is worth noting that only a few poets achieve the status of the omniscient paradigm in each language: Kālidāsa for Sanskrit, Kampaṉ for Tamil, and Tĕnāli Rāmaliṅgaḍu in Telugu (there is also the one instance of Timmana, see above). We have to repeat that despite the fact that these and other poets who appear in the *cāṭu* tradition bear the same names as the poets who authored great books in their respective languages, they are *not* the persons known to the standard textual tradition. In the *cāṭu* tradition, poets become legends. Released from their chronological limitations and biographical boundaries, authors acquire the freedom of existing purely as creators of the poetry attributed to them. Thus it becomes wholly natural for Kālidāsa (fourth century) and Bhavabhūti (eighth century) or Daṇḍin (eighth century) to meet in the *cāṭu* stories, to exchange poems, to offer criticism of one another's work. Indeed, there is a sense in which the *cāṭu* world aims precisely at this effect, bringing major voices into active relation to one another, establishing the dense fabric of intertextual resonances that allows for a new form of literary criticism to emerge.[16]

Within this echo chamber of verses and stories, the tradition

16. There is an affinity here to the kind of literary history projected for Western literatures by David Perkins, *Is Literary History Possible?* (Baltimore: Johns Hopkins University Press, 1993).

also makes judgments about the relative merit of the poets. We will explore some of these statements more deeply in the concluding essay; but to illustrate the point, here is a story which plays with the images of Kālidāsa and Daṇḍin.

These two poets were both patronized by King Bhoja, but the king always showed preference for Kālidāsa. This irritated Daṇḍin. The two poets wanted to settle the issue by referring it to the goddess Sarasvatī, so they set out for her temple. On the way, they came to a beautiful garden, unnoticed before, where a striking young woman was sitting with her maid. They simply could not resist approaching her. Attempting, somewhat lamely, to strike up a conversation, Daṇḍin said:

tūrṇam ānīyatāṃ cūrṇaṃ pūrṇa-candra-nibhânane

O moon-faced beauty:
We need supplies—a little lime
for our betel, fast.

To this half-verse Kālidāsa added:

parṇāni svarṇa-varṇāni karṇântâyata-locane

And a few more leaves, fresh as gold,
long as your matchless eyes.

The young woman—who was the goddess Sarasvatī in disguise—answered this request by addressing her maidservant:

patrāṇi dīyatāṃ cūrṇaṃ pūrṇa-candra-nibhânane
kālidāsāya kavaye daṇḍine paṇḍitāya ca

Give some betel leaves and lime,
O moon-faced beauty,
to Kālidāsa, the poet,
and to Pandit Daṇḍin.

The goddess unerringly identifies the superior poet by virtue of the lyricism of his line, his delicate taste—he chews only fresh, golden betel leaves—and by the iconically suggestive vocative with which he addresses her, *karṇântâyata-locane* (literally, "whose eyes are long, reaching almost to her ears"). One can almost see her long lashes in the long vowels, and the soft movement of the eyes in the repeated liquids. Daṇḍin, by way of contrast, uses a trite scholarly phrase, which the goddess dryly repeats in addressing her maid. He, too, brings in alliterative long vowels and liquids, but in a mechanical and pedantic way. The difference in style, in the two halves of the poem, is striking: Daṇḍin repeats stock phrases in a prosaic sequence built around a practical request; Kālidāsa builds on the same syllabic configurations, but with a grace and charm that make us aware of the arrestingly beautiful woman in front of him. Unexpectedly, the test has already been settled: the goddess disappears, and Daṇḍin recognizes his defeat.

Subtle touches such as these pervade the *cāṭu* system. The verses themselves, taken together, shaped the sensibility of their audience with their wit, their precision, and their sheer poetic power. Moving from gnomic advice to metalinguistic criticism, through the domains of desire, social commentary, the articulation of cultural values, and critical taste, these interlocking stanzas embody an entire education, an expressive vision of life and poetry.

A poem remembered at the right moment,
however simple,
glows with life.

In making love,
beauty unadorned
is perfect.

avasara-paṭhitā vāṇī guṇa-gaṇa-rahitâpi śobhate puṃsām
rati-samaye ramaṇīnāṃ bhūṣā-hānis tu bhūuṣaṇaṃ bhavati

Samayôcita-padya-mālikā (Bombay, 1941), 1.

Poetic Justice

Condemn me, O Creator,
to any punishment you see fit
for all the sins I've committed.
But the hell of reading poetry
to those who have no taste for it—
not that, not that!

itara-pāpa-phalāni yathêcchayā
vilikhitāni sahe caturânana
arasikāya kavitva-nivedanaṃ
śirasi mā likha mā likha mā likha

Kāmasūtra

It was the very first night,
and the young girl showed surprising skill
in the arts of love—
so much so that her husband held his head
in his hands, a little worried.
But she just laughed and painted a picture
on the wall—a lion cub,
only half-born, already leaping
at an elephant.

nūtana-ḵeḷi bāliḵa manohara-rītula ḵeḷi salpagā
ḍātala ceyi dālci vibhuḍ' anya-vicāramu jĕndiy uṇḍagān
ā taraḷāḵṣi navvi sagam' īnina siṅgamu ḵrindan enugun
nāti liḵhiñci cūpa nija-nāthuḍu santasam' andĕn ĕntayun

There is a Sanskrit version of this *cāṭu*:

> *bālāyā nava-saṅgame caturatāṃ vīḵṣyânyathā-śaṅḵinaḥ*
> *patyuś cittam aveḵṣya sā ca caturā bhittau ḵim apy āliḵhat*
> *ādau matta-gajaṃ tathā tad-upari ḵrodhāt patantaṃ śiśum*
> *siṃhī-garbha-vinirgataṃ tad-ubhayam dṛṣṭvā sa hṛṣṭo 'bhavat*

Cāṭu-dhārā-camatḵāra-sāra, compiled by Allamarāju Subrahmaṇyakavi (Rajamundry: Śrī sujana-rañjanī-mudrâkṣara-śālā, 1931), 71.

Spilled Milk

A prince came galloping on horseback into a small town. A group of milkmaids scattered at his approach; their pots of curds fell and broke. They began crying at this loss, except for one, who started laughing. Asked by the prince to explain, she gave this account of her life:

First I killed the king.
Then my husband died of snakebite.
Tortured by hunger, I went to an alien town
and sold my body, amassing sin.
But when I saw my own son
come to me as a customer,
I couldn't bear it, tried to burn myself
and failed. Now I sell curds.
Why cry, King,
if they spill?

bhūpati jampitin magaḍu bhūri bhujaṅgamuceta caccĕ
tān ākaṭa kundi kundi udayārkuni paṭṭaṇam egi veśyanai
pāpamu gaṭṭikoṇṭin' aṭa paṭṭi viṭuṇḍ'ayi rāga jūci san-
tāpamu jĕndi aggi vaḍi dagdhamugāk' iṭu gŏlla-bhāmanai
ī panik' ŏppu-koṇṭi nṛpatī vagap' eṭiki calla cindinan

This verse is the central text of a long folk narrative, later made into a Telugu movie called *Gŏlla-bhāma*, "Cowherdess."

Knots

They say a woman has five knots.
Two are forced open by her husband.
One comes loose by her liking.
The last two let go
in making love.

satik' aidu muḷḷu kalav' aṭa
paticetanu rĕṇḍu muḷḷu balimini vīḍun
hitamatin ŏka muḍi vīḍunu
rati seyaga rĕṇḍu muḷḷu ramaṇiki vīḍun

The first two knots are apparently those that tie the blouse and the sari. The third is a voluntary mental movement.

Not Entirely Hidden

Not entirely hidden,
like the enormous breasts of those Gujarati women,
and not open to view,
like a Tamil woman's breasts,
but rather,
like the supple, half-uncovered breasts
of a Telugu girl,
neither concealed nor exposed:

that's how a poem should be composed.
Anything else
is a joke.

ghanatara-ghūrjarī-kuca-yuga-kriya gūḍhamu gāka drāviḍī-
stana-gati teṭa gāka aracāṭ' agu āndhra-vadhūṭi cŏkkapun
canu-gava-līla gūḍhatayu cāṭutanambunu lekay uṇḍa cĕp-
pinan adipo kavitvam' anipiñcu nagiñc' aṭugākay uṇḍinan

A Definition of Poetry

Is poetry a surface sheen,
the green delusion of unfolded buds?
It must be real inside
and out, exploding fragrance,
an aching touch your body can't forget
by day or night, like of your woman,
whenever you think about it.
It should come over you, it should murmur
deep in the throat, as your lover in her dovelike moaning,
and as you listen, yearning comes in all its beauty.
If you take hold of it, your fingers tingle
as if you were tracing the still-hidden breasts
of a young girl, wholly embraced.
If you sink your teeth into it, it should be succulent
as the full lips of a ripe woman from another world,
sitting on your knees. It should ring
as when godly Sound strokes with her fingernails
the strings of her *vīṇā*, with its golden bulbs resting
on her proud, white, pointed breasts,
so that the *rāga*-notes resound.
That is the pure Telugu mode.
If you use Sanskrit, then a rushing, gushing
overflow of moonlight waves, luminous and cool,
from Śiva's crest, the mountain-born goddess beside him,
enveloping actors and their works, the dramas
spoken by Speech herself in the presence of the Golden Seed,

pounding out the powerful rhythms, the beat
of being, through drums and strings
and chiming bells and thousands of ringing anklets
dancing, drawing out the words, the fragrant and subtle
winds wafting essence of unfolding lotus
from the Ganges streaming in the sky should
comfort your mind. You should shiver
in pleasure again and again, each time
you hear it, as rivulets of honeyed juices and butter
and sweet milk flow together
and mix their goodness more and more
and more.

pūta mĕruṅgulun pasaru pūpabĕḍaṅgulu cūpanaṭṭiv' ā
ḳaitalu jaggu niggu nĕna gāvalĕ gammuna gamm'anan-valen
rātiriyun baval marapurāni hŏyal cĕliy ārajampu nid-
dā-taritīpuloy anaga tārasilan-vale lo dalañcinan
bātiga paiḳŏnan-valĕnu paidali ḳuttuḳaloni pallaṭī
ḳūtal'anan-valĕn sŏgasu ḳorḳulu rā-valĕn ālaḳiñcinan
cetiḳŏlandi ḳaugiṭanu jercina ḳanniya cinni pŏnni mel
mūtala cannu-doyi-vale muccaṭa gāvale paṭṭi cūcinan
ḍātoḍan'unna minnula miṭārapu muddula gumma ḳamman'au
vātĕra dŏṇḍa-paṇḍuvalĕ vācavi-gāvalĕ paṇṭan ūdinan
ḳātala tammicūli-dora ḳaivasapun javarāli sibbĕpun
metĕliy abburampu jigi nibbarap' ubbagu gabbi-gubba pon-
būtalan unna ḳāyasari poḍimi ḳinnĕra melubanti san-
gātapu sanna-tanti bayaḳārapu ḳannaḍa-gauḷa-pantuḳā-
sātata-tāna-tānala-pasand' ivuṭāḍĕḍu goṭa mīṭu bal

mrotalunun-balĕn haruvu mŏllamu gāvalĕn accatĕṅgul ī rītiga —

saṃskṛtamb' upacariñcĕḍu paṭṭuna bhāratī-vadhū-
ṭī-tapanīya-garbha-nikaṭī-bhavad-ānana-parva-sāhitī-
śita-nagātmajā-giriśa-śekhara-śīta-mayūkha-rekhikâ-
pāta-sudhā-prapūra-bahu-bhaṅga-ghumaṃ-ghuma-
ghuṃghumārbhaṭī-jātaka-tāḷa-yugma-laya-saṅgati-cuñcu-vipañcikā-mṛdan-
gâtata-tehi-tat-tahita-hādhita-dhim-dhaṇu-dhaṇu-dhim-dhimi-
vrāta-nayânukūla-pada-vāra-kuhūdvaha-hāri-kiṅkiṇī-
nūtana-ghalghalâcaraṇa-nūpura-jhāḷajhaḷī-maranda-saṅ-
ghāta-viyad-dhunī-cakacakad-vikacôtpala-sāra-saṅgrahâ-
yāta-kumāra-gandhavaha-hāri-sugandha-vilāsa-yuktamai
cetamu calla-jeya-valĕ jill'ana jalla-valĕn manohara-
dyotaka-gostanī-phala-madhu-drava-goghṛta-pāyasa-prasā-
dâtirasa-prasara-rucira-prasaraṃbuga sārĕ sārĕkun.

This verse in *utpala-māla* meter is ascribed to Pĕddana. One day the king, Kṛṣṇadevarāya, brought a golden anklet (*gaṇḍa-pĕṇḍeramu*) to the court and promised to give it to any poet who could compose equally well in Telugu and Sanskrit. Pĕddana spontaneously sang the verse and was rewarded with the anklet, which the king himself placed around the poet's foot. Pĕddana refers to this moment in the poem he composed for Kṛṣṇadevarāya upon the king's death. See page 69, "A Poet's Lament."

Logical Proof

The great logician Udayanâcārya, a specialist in ontological arguments, arrived in Puri to visit Lord Jagannātha, but found the temple closing for the day. In anger he addressed the god:

You're so drunk on wealth and power
that you ignore my presence.
Just wait: when the Buddhists come,
your whole existence
depends on me.

aiśvarya-mada-matto 'si mām avajñāya vartase
upasthiteṣu bauddheṣu mad-adhīnā tava sthitiḥ

J. Prabhakara Sastry recalled this verse.

Why People Fall Asleep at Conferences

Kumbhakarṇa loved Sleep.
After Rāma killed him in battle,
Sleep was widowed.
Since then, she spends her time
at lectures.

nidrā-priyo yaḥ khalu kumbhakarṇo
hataḥ samīke sa raghūttamena
vaidhavyam āpadyata tasya bhāryā
śrotuṃ samāyāti kathā-purāṇam

Kumbhakarṇa, the demon Rāvaṇa's brother, used to sleep six months a year. Widows often attend religious discourses.

Ashok Aklujkar recited this verse.

Mutual Admiration

When a camel gets married,
the donkey performs the wedding.
Each praises the other:
"What a beauty!" "What a voice!"

uṣṭrasya lagna-velāyāṃ
gārdabhaḥ stuti-pāṭhakaḥ
parasparaṃ praśaṃsanti
aho rūpam aho dhvaniḥ

We thank Padmanabh Jaini for this verse.

The Other Tongue

The village elders gather on the porch of the Rāma temple
to recite *Mahābhārata* and talk of other things.

"Telugu is a good language," they say.
"This hissing-spitting *Engilis* that our boys are speaking
goes no farther than their lips,
even if they pass F.A., B.A., or some other A."

mudi karaṇāḷu rāmu-guḍi-mosala raccalu dīrci bhāratāl
caduvucu loka-vārtala-praśaṃsalan aṇḍru tĕluṅgu bāsa mañ-
cidi mana pillakāyalu vaciñcĕḍiy ingilipīsu pus-pusan
pĕdavulu dāṭad' ĕntaṭi yĕfeyu biye yĕmiye vaciñcinan

This *cāṭu* has an author: Dāsu Śrīrāmulu (Eluru, 1846–1908).

A Single Thought

Total knowledge belongs to God.
What human beings know
is rather slight.
There's not much reason to be proud.
Attacking others will never make you free.
You have to sift through many rocks
to find one gem.
One strong thought is enough
if you think it through.

sarvajñatvamu sāmbamūrtidi manuṣya-prajñay alpambu dur-
garvambul koragāvu dūṣaṇala mokṣa-śrīlu cekurav' īy-
urvin khānikuḍ' ĕnni rāḷḷu vaḍapoyun ratnam' ŏkkaṇṭikai
gurv-arthamb' ŏkaḍ' unna cāladĕ sudhī-kumbhul vicāriñcinan

Cĕllapilla Veṅkaṭa Śāstri supplied this verse by Dāsu Śrīrāmulu from memory when a second printed collection of the latter's poetry was being prepared. See the preface to Dāsu Śrīrāmulu's *Tĕlugunāḍu* (6th printing, Hyderabad: Mahākavi dāsu śrīrāmulu smāraka samiti, 1974).

A Goose among Herons

"Who are you, Red-Face, Red-Feet?"
"I'm a goose."
"Where do you live?"
"Far away, in Mānasa Lake."
"Tell us something about it."
"It's full of golden lotuses and lovely pearls."
"What about snails?"
"Never heard of them."

So said the noble bird,
and the herons sneered: "Aha!"

ěvvaḍav' īvu k̨āḷḷu mŏgam' ěrrana haṃsaman' ěnduṇ' unduvo
davvula mānasambunanu dāna viśeṣamul' emi tělpumā
mavvapu k̨āñcanâbjamulu mauk̨tik̨amul k̨alav' andu nattalo
avvi ěrumgan' annan ahahāy ani navvě bak̨ambul anniyun

This somewhat cryptic conversation may be an *anyâpadeśa*—an exercise in oblique reference to someone or something outside the verse. In this case, the goose would be a real poet surrounded by philistines. Another possibility is that the goose, given to the high life, fails to notice the ordinary reality in front of him.

On the Ball

One day King Bhoja was walking through the courtesan streets when he saw a young woman playing ball. In the flurry of play, the lotus flower from her hair had fallen to the ground. He returned to his court and asked his poets to produce a verse about the game. Bhavabhūti began:

I know what you're after:
a stolen kiss from her lips.
That's why, pushed away
by her lotus-red hand,
time after time
you keep bouncing back.

viditaṃ nanu kanduka te hṛdayam
pramadâdhara-saṅgama-lubdha iva
vanitā-kara-tāmarasâbhihataḥ
patitaḥ patitaḥ punar utpatasi

Vararuci continued:

This one ball looks like three.
Touching her palm,
it's red as red can be.
On the ground, in the gleam
of her toenails, it's white as white.

In the space between, caught by her eyes,
it's darker than the dark.

eko 'pi traya iva bhāti kanduko 'yam
kāntāyāḥ kara-tala-rāga-rakta-raktaḥ
bhūmau tac-caraṇa-nakhâṃśu-gaura-gauraḥ
khasthaḥ san nayana-marīci-nīla-nilaḥ

Kālidāsa concluded:

The lotus is worried.
"Why is she hitting this ball?
Is she mad at it
for looking like her breasts?
But I look like her eyes!"

In a panic,
it falls pleading
at her feet.

payodharâkāra-dharo hi kandukaḥ
kareṇa roṣād abhihanyate muhuḥ
itîva netrâkṛti-bhītam utpalam
striyaḥ prasādāya papāta pādayoḥ

The King gave each of the poets one hundred thousand rupees per syllable, but he especially honored Kālidāsa, who knew about the fallen lotus.

Red, White, and Blue

In Sītā's hands, perfect as the red lotus,
they're rubies.
On Rāma's head, they're white
as jasmine buds.
Pouring down his luminous dark body, they're blue
as sapphires.

May you be blessed
with Rāma's wedding pearls.

jānakyāḥ kamalâmalāñjali-puṭeḥ yāḥ padma-rāgāyitāḥ
nyastā rāghava-mastake ca vilasat-kunda-prasūnāyitāḥ
srastāḥ śyāmala-kāya-kānti-kalitā yā indranīlāyitāḥ
muktās tāḥ śubhadā bhavantu bhavatāṃ śrīrāma-vaivāhikāḥ

This *cāṭu* is often printed on wedding invitations.

Color-Blind Critics

I'm Vijjikā,
dark as the silken petal of the black lily,
and Daṇḍin doesn't know me.

How stupid
to claim the Goddess of Poetry
is white!

nīlotpala-dala-śyāmāṃ vijjikāṃ māṃ ajānatā
vṛthâiva daṇḍinā proktaṃ sarva-śuklā sarasvatī

The great poetician Daṇḍin describes Sarasvatī, Goddess of Poetry, as *sarva-śuklā*, "entirely white," in the opening verse of his *Kāvyâdarśa*. The *cāṭu* verse, commenting on this attribution, is ascribed to a queen-poetess called Vijjikā.

New Age

They now read proofs at printing shops
just to stay alive,
or teach Telugu to the white Huns,
expound religion in the houses
of those grocers who give them credit.
Phenomenal scholars have been humbled.
Times have changed.

accāphīsul' aṭañcu hūṇulak' upādhyāyatvam' añcun marin
vĕccamb' iccĕḍi baccuṭiṇḍulakaḍan vedântam' añcun mahô-
dyaccāritrulu paṇḍitul mĕlganayyĕn gadā pŏṭṭakai
caccuṅ-gālamu vaccĕ gauravamu nāśamb' ayyĕ kāmeśvarī

This *cāṭu* is originally from Cĕllapilla Veṅkaṭa Śāstri's *Kāmeśvarī-śatakamu.*

Real Words

Five, four, three,
and the one, beyond all knowledge,
that flows through them all—

it belongs
in a distant tongue
in this temple of Kurukūr,
or so they say,

but as for me, it's all there
in my mother tongue.

aimpŏruḷum nāṟpŏruḷum muppŏruḷum pĕyt'amaitta
cĕmpŏruḷai ĕmmaṟaikkum cetpŏruḷait taṇkurukūrc
ceymŏḻiya t'ĕṉpar cilariyāṉ ivvulakil
tāymŏḻiya t'ĕṉpeṉ takaintu

Five elements, four goals of human life, the three great gods—Śiva, Viṣṇu, Brahmā—all these are externalizations of true being (*pŏruḷ*) identified as the god at the temple of Tirukkurukūr. When the poetess Auvaiyār arrived there, she was drawn into a discussion about the relative merits of Sanskrit and Tamil in the liturgy. This verse is her response.

City of Poets

King Vikramârka exiled from his city anyone who could not compose poetry. A weaver is said to have uttered this verse in response.

I can make poems.
I can't make them very good.
If I work at it, I'll make them good.
You're a conquering king, your enemies
surrender crowns at your feet.
What, then, do you want from me?
I can achieve poetry,
weave,
or leave.

k̨āvyaṃ k̨aromi na hi cārutaraṃ k̨aromi
yatnāt k̨aromi yadi cārutaraṃ k̨aromi
bhūpāla-mauli-maṇi-maṇḍana-pada-pīṭha
he sāhasâṅk̨a k̨avayāmi vayāmi yāmi

The final three verbs show a progressive omission of prior syllables: *k̨avayāmi*, "I compose poetry > *vayāmi*, "I weave > *yāmi*, "I go." Such a series is considered an ornament of sound (*śabdâlaṅk̨āra*) in Sanskrit poetics; the weaver's protest thus nicely reveals his verbal skill. The root "to weave" is also used for composing poetry.

We thank J. Prabhakara Sastry for quoting this verse.

Fault Lines?

In the old days, if a text was demanding,
the reader felt it was *his* lack.
These days the poet is to blame.
Devious are the ways
of this dying age.

tŏlināḷula padyārthamu
tĕliyanico pāṭhakunidi tĕliyami. ī nā-
ḷula vrāsina kavi doṣamu.
kali gaḍacina kŏladi citra-gatulan cĕlagun

The great twentieth-century poet Viśvanātha Satyanārāyaṇa (d. 1976) composed this verse in response to Marxist and other modern critics, who accused him of being opaque.

Hard to Crack

Torture us, please,
impossible poet,
with your exuberance of stunning words
and delicious feeling slightly mixed
with bitter dryness. We need jaws of stone
to grind the elevated phrases you utter with ease
as you tease us through your labyrinths,
books cooked to the texture of rock.

kiñcit-tikta-kaṣāya-ṣāḍaba-rasa-kṣepātirekâtivāk-
sañcāra-pracayâvakāśamulalo kavy-udgha gaṇḍâśmamul
cañcal-līlan udātta-vāg-garimato sādhiñci vedhiñcumā
pañcāriñci pravahlikā-kṛta-kṛtin pāṣāna-pāka-prabhū

This verse was composed by Jalasūtram Rukmiṇīnātha Śāstri ("Jaruk" Śāstri) in ironic praise of the great Viśvanātha Satyanārāyaṇa, whom he regarded as his guru. The texture of rock (*pāṣāṇa-pāka*) is a parodic addition to the well-known three textures (*pāka*, literally, "cooking to a certain consistency") of poetry: *drākṣā-pāka*, "the grape," which is savored without effort; *kadaḷī-pāka*, "the banana," which requires peeling before tasting; and *narikeḷa-pāka*, "the coconut," where the thick fibrous exterior has to be removed and then the hard nut broken open.

What's in a Name

One day Bhoja quarreled with Kālidāsa; in his anger, the king called the poet "a rotten bastard" (*bhraṣṭa*). The next day, Kālidāsa dressed himself as a monk, with meat in his begging bowl. When the king saw him, the following conversation took place:

"Should a monk be eating meat?"
"Certainly not—unless you have wine to go with it."
"So you drink, too?"
"With gusto, if I have a woman."
"Where do you get the money to pay a whore?"
"I gamble or I steal."
"So your holiness is good at dice and thieving?"
"What else can a rotten bastard do?"

bhikṣo māṃsa-niṣevanaṃ kim ucitaṃ? kim tena madyaṃ vinā?
madyaṃ câpi tava priyaṃ? priyam aho vārâṅganābhis saha.
vāra-strī-rataye kutas tava dhanaṃ? dyūtena cauryeṇa vā.
caurya-dyūta-pariśramo 'sti bhavatāṃ? bhraṣṭasya kā vā gatiḥ?

The last line gave away the disguise; the contrite king invited Kālidāsa back to his court.

Poetry Juice

King Bhoja saw Kālidāsa carrying a big fish under his arm. A conversation ensued:

"What's that thing under your arm?"
"It's a book."
"Why is it dripping?"
"Must be an overflow of poetry juice."
"So why does it stink?"
"Probably the corpses left behind
when Rāma fought Rāvaṇa to the death."
"But it has a tail!"
"It's written on palm leaves, not yet trimmed."
"So what book is it, honored poet?"
"My lord, it's the one even Brahmins relish,
that fishy tale about God."

kakṣe kiṃ tava? pustakaṃ. kim udakam? kāvyârtha-sārôdakam.
gandhaḥ kiṃ? nanu rāma-rāvaṇa-mahā-saṅgrāma-raṅgôdbhavaḥ?
pucchaḥ kiṃ? nanu tāla-patra-likhitaṃ? kiṃ pustakaṃ bho kave?
rājan bhūmi-suraiś ca sevitam idaṃ rāmāyaṇaṃ pustakam.

When the king demanded to see for himself, the fish had turned into a book. (Brahmins do not eat fish; as a learned poet, Kālidāsa is expected to be vegetarian.)

A Switch in Time

The poet Bhaṭṭumūrti, whom tradition places in Kṛṣṇadevarāya's court, became angry with the king's famous minister, Timmarasu. He began singing the following poem about him, highlighting Timmarasu's lowly origins:

He used to sew leaves together in Gutti
for serving plates. In Candragiri he begged
for food. He lived on handouts
from the soup kitchen of Penugonda.
He carried betel leaves in a bag
for little kings in local forts. Upstarts like him—

guttin pullĕlu kuṭṭi candragirilo kūḍ'ĕtti pĕngŏṇḍalo
hattin satramun andu vedi palu durgādhīśu tāmbūlapun
tittul mosi padasthulaina ghanulan—

At this point, seeing what was coming, Timmarasu hurriedly took the pearl necklace from his neck and presented it to the poet, who now completed the verse:

  are no subject for *my* poem. I'd rather sing
of Nāgama's son, Timma, masterful minister,
slayer of foes.

dīvimpa diviñcĕdan
mattārāti-yayāti-nāgama-sutun mantrīśvarun timmarun

A Poem by Committee: The Dawn

King Bhoja gave the following line to his poets as *samasyā*—to be completed as a four-line poem:

carama-giri-nitambe candrabimbaṃ lalambe

The Moon rests his head in the lap of the Western sky.

First Bhavabhūti produced a line:

aruṇa-kiraṇa-jālair antarikṣe gatarkṣe

In the red glow of morning, stars fade from heaven.

Then Daṇḍin added his line:

calati śiśira-vāte manda-mandaṃ prabhāte

A cooling breeze moves through the dawn like a sigh.

Now Kālidāsa finished the verse by adding the third line:

yuvati-jana-kadambe nātha-muktoṣṭha-bimbe

Lovers leave one last kiss on the lips of young women.

The full poem now reads:

In the red glow of morning, stars fade from heaven.
A cooling breeze moves through the dawn like a sigh.
Lovers leave one last kiss on the lips of young women
as the Moon rests his head in the lap of the Western sky.

A Day in the Life of an Executive

Mornings are for churning oceans.
You are roped to the stake,
with the wind for breakfast.
Evenings you have to hold the whole world
on your head.
Here in Cĕnturutti,
paddy fields rippling with pearls,
you grace the chest of the god
whose body never lies.
Is this the hour of your rest?

kālaiyilum velai kaṭaiyak kayiṟ' ākum
mālaiyilum pūmuṭittu vāḻume—colaicĕṟi
cĕyyil āram payilum cĕnturutti mānakarvāḻ
pŏyillā mĕyyar iṭum pūṇ

The verse, attributed to Kāḷamekappulavar, describes the great serpent Ādiśeṣa—here identified with the snake that adorns the body of Śiva in his shrine at Tirutturutti. When the ocean of milk was churned by the gods and the demons, a great snake served as the rope coiled around Mount Mandara, the churning-rod. Ādiśeṣa is said to bear the earth on his head. Puns color the description: for example, *kālaiyilum*, "in the morning," is also *kāl-ayilum*, "eating wind," that is, a snake (snakes feed on air).

Dead Poets Beware

King Vīrā-rĕḍḍi has merged into God.
Who will give me jewels and clothes?
Mailāru of the Panta family has moved to God's mountain.
What king will pay me my per diem?
Rāhuttu, the Telugu king, sleeps with the courtesans in
the sky.
What king will give me musk in exchange for a poem?
Vissana, the prime minister, lives in the other world.
Who will wine me and dine me on plates of gold?
Bhāskara long ago met his maker.
It's hard to go on living in this dying age.
Now it's time for the poets in heaven
to shake in terror: Śrīnātha, the Undefeated,
is on his way.

k̨āśik̨a-viśveśu galasĕ vīrā-rĕḍḍi
ratnāmbarambul' e-rāyaḍ' iccu
k̨ailāsagiri panṭa mailāru-vibhuḍ' unḍĕ
dina-vĕccam' e-rāju tīrpa-galaḍu
rambha gūḍĕ tĕnuṅgu-rāya-rāhuttunḍu
k̨astūrik̨' e'rāju prastutintu
svarga-sthuḍ' ayyĕ vissana-mantri mari hema-
pātrânnam' ĕvvani paṅk̨ti k̨aladu
bhāsk̨aruḍu munnĕ devuni pālik̨' arigĕ
k̨aliyugambunan ik̨an unḍa k̨aṣṭam' anucu
divija-k̨avi-varu-gunḍiyal diggur' anagan
aruguccunnāḍu śrīnathuḍ' amara-purik̨i

Legend says that Śrīnātha uttered this verse just before he died. He mentions the names of his former patrons, all dead before him.

Back to Me

Full red lips, breasts, curls,
darting eyes that steal the heart:
so what if you show me
none of these, what if
you turn the other way?
Can't I make do
with your curved and ravishing behind
and your coiled braid?
Is there merit on one side of the river
and no fun on the other side
when the full moon flashes in water
like your smile?

vara-bimbâdharamun payodharamulun vakrâlakambul mano-
hara-lolâkṣulu cūpak' avvali mŏgamb' ainantan em' āyĕ? nī
guru-bhāsvaj-jaghanambu krŏmmuḍiyu mākuñ cālave? gaṅgak' ad-
dari mel' iddari kīḍunun kaladĕ? udyad-rāja-bimbânanā

This verse is ascribed to Tĕnāli Rāmaliṅgaḍu, addressing a woman turned away from him in bed.

Good Taste

Music and poetry:
the Goddess of Arts has two breasts.
One is delicious at first tasting.
The other becomes so
when you chew on it.

saṅgītaṃ sāhityaṃ ca sarasvatyāḥ stana-dvayam
ekam āpāta-madhuram anyad ālocanâmṛtam

This poem reinterprets two key terms of Sanskrit poetic theory: *āsvādana*, "savoring," and *carvaṇā*, "chewing." Both terms mean "enjoyment of the taste or feeling (*rasa*) of a good poem." The *cāṭu*, however, draws an important distinction between two kinds of aesthetic enjoyment—one effortless and spontaneous, the other requiring a more sustained process of working at it.

How to Tame a Pandit

A Sanskrit scholar came to Kṛṣṇadevarāya's court and, impatient with the Telugu poems sung there, complained:

āndhra-bhāṣā-mayaṃ kāvyam ayo-maya-vibhūṣaṇam

A poem made out of Telugu
is like a necklace made out of iron—

Tĕnāli Rāmaliṅgaḍu completed the verse as follows:

saṃskṛtâraṇya-sañcāri-vidvan-mattêbha-śṛṅkhalam

a perfect chain to restrain
pandits prowling like wild elephants
through the Sanskrit jungle trails.

Win a Mustache

In the early decades of this century, two poets—Divākarla Tirupati Śāstri and Cĕllapilla Veṅkaṭa Śāstri—teamed up to perform stunning feats of oral versification, improvisation, and memory. As a pair, they became known as Tirupati-Veṅkaṭa Kavulu; immensely popular, they traveled through Andhra like conquering kings, challenging poets to contests and receiving honors from local zamindars. Although both of them were Vaidika Brahmins, they sported mustaches like those worn by men from more power-oriented castes (such as Niyogis, Velamas, and Reddis). Once, during one of their performances, someone in the audience questioned them about this. Here is the response they improvised on the spot:

We knew it's wrong to grow a mustache,
but we did it anyway, heedless
of the rules, to show that we
are master poets in both languages.*
If your pride is hurt, O great poets,
come and defeat us. If you win,
we'll shave off our mustaches
and throw them at your feet
with the respect you deserve.

doṣam' aṭañc' ĕriṅgiyunu dunduḍuḵ' ŏppaga pĕñcināram' ī
mīsalu rĕṇḍu bāsalaḵu memĕ ḵavîndrulam' añcu tĕlpagā
roṣamu ḵalginan ḵavi-varul mamu gĕlvuḍu gĕltureni ī
mīsalu tīsi mī pada-samīpamunan paḍavaici mrŏḵḵame

*Telugu and Sanskrit.

Basic Necessities

Kālidāsa's poems,
milk and curds,
antelope meat
and a young woman:

if I have these—and youthful vigor—
I can go on
life after life.

kālidāsa-kavitā navaṃ vayaḥ
māhiṣaṃ dadhi sa-śarkaraṃ payaḥ
aiṇa-māṃsam abalā ca komalā
sambhavantu mama janma-janmani

Survival of the Fittest

Saṅkusāla Nṛsiṃhakavi composed this verse and sold it for four thousand golden coins to Mohanâṅgi, the daughter of Kṛṣṇadevarāya. While playing chess with her father, Mohanâṅgi found herself caught between two powerful pieces (the minister and the elephant). As she was trying to extricate herself from this situation, she recited the final line of this verse:

Pressured by the hips from below
and the ample breasts from above,
this woman's scanty waist
must have run away.
If it were still there,
you could surely see it.
Hemmed in by superpowers,
how can the weak survive?

ottuk̲ŏni vaccu k̲aṭi-k̲ucôdvṛtti cūci
taruṇi tanu-madhyam' ĕcaṭik̲'o talagi poyĕ
uṇḍĕneniyu k̲anabaḍak̲unnĕn ahaha
uddhatula madhya pedalak̲' uṇḍa taramĕ

The king asked to hear the rest of the verse and the name of the author. Nṛsiṃhakavi was rewarded. They say that this poet, the author of the *Kavi-k̲arṇa-rasâyaṇamu*, where the verse appears (3.26), had earlier tried to see the king but was prevented from doing so by Pĕddana, who was afraid of being superseded.

Some say that when the king discovered that he had neglected a great poet, he composed the *Āmuktamālyada* in atonement. Another version is that the king made Pĕddana compose the *Āmukta-mālyada*, in the king's name, as a punishment. Medieval Telugu poets conventionally describe the woman's waist as thin to the point of invisibility.

Grammar School

They taught me "it" was neuter,
so I sent off my mind to my girlfriend.
Now it's making love to her
and won't come back.
Never trust a linguist.

napuṃsakam iti jñātvā priyāyai preṣitaṃ manaḥ
tat tu tatrâiva ramate hatāḥ pāṇininā vayam

A Poet's Lament

When he would see me on the street,
he would halt his elephant
and help me up with his own hand.
For the mere asking, he gave me villages
like Kokata, in any region.
On the day I dedicated my *Story of Manu* to him,
he himself carried the palanquin where I was seated.
He told me I alone was worthy to wear the anklet
of a triumphant poet, and it was he who tied it on my foot.
He called me Doyen of Telugu Poetry, Allasāni Pĕddana,
King of Poets.

Now Kṛṣṇarāya has died, and I couldn't go with him
to heaven. I stay on,
like the living dead.

edur'aina co tana mada-k̲arîndramu nilpi
k̲elūtay ŏsagiy ĕk̲k̲iñcu k̲ŏniyĕ
k̲ok̲ata-gramādy-anek̲âgrahārambul'
aḍigina sīmalayandun iccĕ
manucaritramb' andu-k̲ŏnu veḷa puram' ega
pallak̲i tana k̲ela baṭṭi ettĕ
birudaina k̲avi-gaṇḍa-pĕṇḍeramunak̲' īvĕ
tagud' ani tāne padamuna tŏḍigĕ
āndhra-k̲avitā-pitāmaha allasāni
pĕddana k̲avîndra ani nannu pilucunaṭṭi
k̲ṛṣṇa-rāyala-to divik̲' egalek̲a
bratik̲iy unnāḍa jīvacchavamban agucu

For the story of the anklet given by Kṛṣṇadevarāya to Pĕddana, see pages 34–36, "A Definition of Poetry." *The Story of Manu* (*Manu-caritramu*) is Pĕddana's great poem, dedicated to Kṛṣṇadevarāya.

Lament (2)

Go to hell, damned Creator,
you bloodthirsty monster!
Hollow misers
you never touch, but Malkibharāma,
our noble king, so rich in fame—
him you have slain.
Where can poets go for help?
Can you ever make again
someone like him?

rāra vidhāta ori vinarā tagurā talakŏṭlamāri nis-
sārapu-lobhi-rājulanu campaka malkibharāma bhûvarun
cāru-yaśodhanun suguṇi campitiv' arthulak' emi dikku rā
cerikan inta rājunu sṛjimpaga nī taramā vasundharan

This lament is by an anonymous poet associated with the court of the great patron of Telugu letters known as Malkibharāma—the Muslim king of Golconda, Malik Ibrahim Qutubshah (1550–80).

Beauty and the Beast

Full round breasts, body tender as a bud,
limbs golden as they move, eyes piercing and proud:
she's irresistible, this Kāpu woman.
Did you have to give her a tiger
for a husband? You're the Creator,
and I shouldn't blame an elder,
but why should a simple housewife
be so damned attractive?

gubbala gumma lejiguru k̡ŏmma suvarṇapu k̡ilubŏmma bal
gabbi miṭāri cūpuladi k̡āpudi dānik̡in elan ŏk̡k̡anin
bĕbbulin aṇṭa-gaṭṭitivi? pĕddavu ninn' ana rādu k̡āni dān'
abba payojagarbha maganālik̡in inta vilāsam' eṭik̡in?

Ascribed to Śrīnātha, who is addressing Brahmā, the Creator. Kāpus are an agricultural caste; the males are known for their valor and their vigilant protection of their women.

What Lasts?

You'll spend thousands in gold on this splendid sari,
that will wear out within a few months.
Listen, flawless king, famed for spearing
foes in battle:
what *never* wears or tears
is my poem.

nūṟṟupat tāyiram pŏṉpĕṟiṉum nūṟcilai
nāṟṟiṅkaḷ nāḷukkuḷ naintuviṭum—māṟṟalaraip
pŏṉṟap porutaṭakkaipp porvel akaḷaṅka
ĕṉṟum kiḻiyāt'ĕṉ pāṭṭu

Auvaiyār is said to have sung this verse when the Choḻa king failed to pay attention to her because he was busy buying saris for his wife.

A Fair Exchange

I sang of learning, and there was nothing.
I spoke of culture, and there was nothing.
I said he was good, but he was a nothing.
I called him tiger—that good-for-nothing.
I mentioned his muscles, which were nothing.
I praised his charity, and he gave me—nothing.
It's all my fault: words about nothing
get me nothing.

kallāta ŏruvaṉai yāṉ kaṟṟāy ĕṉṟeṉ
kāṭerit tirivaṉai nāṭā ĕṉṟeṉ
pŏllāta ŏruvaṉai nāṉ nallāy ĕṉṟen
pŏrmukattuk kolaiyay yāṉ puliye ĕṉṟeṉ
mallārum puyam ĕṉṟeṉ tempaṟ ṟolai
vaḻaṅkāta kaiyaṉai yāṉ vaḷḷal ĕṉṟeṉ
illātu cŏnneṉukk' illai ĕṉṟāṉ
yāṉum ĕṉṟaṉ kuṟṟattāl ekiṉṟeṉe

Auvaiyār sang this poem when another poet asked her what she had received from a capricious patron. The verse is also attributed to Irāmaccantirak kavirāyar (*Taṉippāṭaṟ-ṟiraṭṭu* 348).

Greetings to My Friends

The monkey on the temple wall,
the priest's pretty wife,
the whore who walks the street,
the wild wind that howls outside—

if you're going to the village,
say hi to them
from me.

guḍi mīdi k̜otitoḍanu
guḍi lopali nambivāri k̜oḍalitoḍan
naḍi-vīthi lañjĕtoḍanu
aḍigŏppula horu gālin aḍigitin' anum̥ā

Ascribed to Śrīnātha, nostalgic for the village of Adigŏppula.

Space to Space

Held-not-held
   by this heap of worms, this body,
the gentle light that is Knowing
   beyond everything that is there,
filling the world without a break,
   not even a hair's breadth in between,
the wholeness that is always first,
   that filters through memory and thought,
an endless goodness closing all gaps
   that brings rich hope to the humble,
unmeasured in words or the movement of the mind,

that one untainted
open space:

enter now
   the space inside me.

yākkaiyĕṉṉum puḻukkurampaiy aṇaint'aṇaiyāp pŏruḷai
aruḷŏḷiyaip parāparattuk k'appuṟamām aṟivai
nīkkamaṟa mayirmuṉaikkum iṭamaṟav ĕṅkĕṅkum niṟaintu
niṉṟa muḻumutalai niṉaivilĕḻuñ cuṭaraip
pākkiyaṅkaḷ cĕyt'aṉantan tavakkuṟaikaṇ muṭikkum
paḻavaṭiyār tamakk'utavum pacuntuṇark kaṟpakattai
vākkumaṉa- vikaṟpattāl-aḷavupaṭāv ŏṉṟai
mācaṟṟa vĕṟuvĕḷiyai maṉavĕḷiyil aṭaippam

This poem was composed by the wife of the poet Varatuṅkarāmapāṇṭiyaṉ at the moment of her death, following closely on that of her husband. He, too, sang a death-poem—a fairly traditional verse of devotion to Śiva. No other poems by this king-poet's wife are known.

Ode to a Donkey

A heap of dust, lusterless and pale,
you roam the neighborhoods of Kondavidu.
Everyone shoos you away.
You lie low in alleyways and corners
and bray.
    By any chance,
are you a poet too?

būḍida-buṅgavaiy oḍalu poḍimi dakki mŏgambu vĕllanai
vāḍala vāḍalan tirigi vārunu vīrunu cŏccŏcoy anan
goḍala gŏndul' and' ŏdigi kūyucun uṇḍĕḍu kŏṇḍavīṭilo
gāḍida nīvunun kavivi kāvu gadāy anumānam' ayyĕḍin

Attributed to Śrīnātha, who found Kondavidu infested with too many poets seeking patrons and being treated with scorn.

Cheaper by the Dozen

Five, six, seven,
eight, nine,
even ten per house
in every village:

poets are popping up everywhere.

As God is my witness, I swear:
once a whole country was lucky
to have one.

devu nāna munnu deśanik' ŏkar' uṇḍa
ippuḍ' ūran ūran inṭan inṭa
evur' ārvur' eḍvur' ĕnamanḍru tŏmmanḍru
padugur' eśi kavulu padmanābha

Drowning

Let the Love God aim his arrows
at me. I don't care.
Let him attack me, with his flag unfurled.
I'll tell the truth, loud and clear.
Whenever that wide-eyed girl looks at me,
there's a flood: the lotuses are up to their neck,
and the fish are in over their heads.

cittajuḍ' algi tūpu mŏna cesina ceyagan immu pai dhvajamb'
ĕttinan ĕttan immu vaciyiñcĕda ḵalgina māṭa gaṭṭigā
attaraḷāyatêḵṣaṇa-ḵaṭāḵṣa-vilāsa-rasa-pravāhamul
ḵuttuḵa-baṇṭi tāmaralaḵun tala-muṅḵalu gaṇḍu-mīlaḵun

The eyes of a beautiful woman are conventionally compared to lotus flowers or to darting fish.

Whitewash

Bhoja's brilliant fame keeps spreading.
Soon the whole universe will be white.
But the more it spreads, the more I'm worried.
What will happen to my lover's hair?

yathā yathā bhoja-yaśo vivardhate
sitāṃ trilokīṃ iva kartum udyatam
tathā tathā me hṛdayaṃ vidūyate
priyâlakâlī-dhavalatva-śaṅkayā

Fame, *yaśas*, is always considered to be white. The verse is attributed to a poet called Śaṅkara (*Bhoja-prabandha* 76).

Like Day and Night

One day Bhoja, walking through his city, observed an elderly Brahmin feeding the Vaiśvadeva offering to the crows. One of these crows cawed loudly, and the Brahmin's young wife fainted in fear. The husband asked why she was afraid, and she replied: "Chaste wives like me are unable to bear harsh noises." Hearing this, the king thought to himself: "This woman, who praises her own chastity, is only pretending to be afraid. Tonight she will certainly do something truly terrible." So at midnight Bhoja returned and secretly followed the woman as she stole out of her house and, carrying a basket filled with meat, proceeded to the bank of the Narmadā River. When crocodiles emerged to attack her, she threw handfuls of meat at them and, having thus diverted their attention, swam safely to the other shore. There she met and made love to her lover, who was impaled on a stake. The king returned to his palace, horrified and amazed. In the morning he said to Kālidāsa:

divā kāka-rutād bhītā

In broad daylight, she's scared of a crow.

Kālidāsa continued:

rātrau tarati narmadām

At night, she swims the river—

The king added:

tatra santi jale grāhāḥ

Swarming with crocodiles!

The poet now completed the verse:

marmajñā sâiva sundarī

Beauty has its wiles.

In final form, the poem thus reads:

In broad daylight, she's scared of a crow.
At night, she swims the river,
swarming with crocodiles.
Beauty has its wiles.

Oral versions speak only of a nocturnal tryst across the river; the bizarre motif of impalement seems to be limited to the recorded Sanskrit text. The verse is often quoted today to imply that women are far from weak when intent upon their own satisfaction (*Bhoja-prabandha* 296).

Philosophers

They're penetrating and profound
in their discussions, those awesome
scholars of Rajahmundry,
tirelessly trying to render judgment

whether through contingent destruction of a prior existent
or *a priori* nonexistence and consequent nonappearance

as in the case, *e.g.*, of flowers
growing in the sky,

at the very source of the Tree of Life,
with its brilliant roots, its branches and leaves
unfolding from a delectable
woman's body, down below,

there is, or is not, evidence
of pubic hair.

haṃsīyānaḵu bhāmaḵun adhama-romāḷul nabhaḥ-puṣpamul
saṃsāra-druma-mūla-pallava-guḷucchamb'aina accoṭa vid-
vāṃsul rājamahêndra-paṭṭaṇamunan dharmâsanamb' uṇḍi pradh-
vāṃsâbhāvamu prāg-abhāvam' anucun carciṃtur' aśrāntamun

Ascribed to Śrīnātha, who is said to have felt contempt for the learned pandits of Rajahmundry. Andhra women shaved off their pubic hairs after puberty. The verse is built around the ironic use of technical Sanskrit terms from the domain of formal logic (*pradhvaṃsâbhāva, prāg-abhāva*).

On Being Full

King Bhoja asked both Bhavabhūti and Kālidāsa to improvise a stanza on the subject of *ratyanta*—the end of love. Here is Bhavabhūti's verse:

muktābhūṣaṇam indu-bimbam ajani vyākīrṇa-tāraṃ nabhaḥ
smāraṃ cāpam apeta-cāpalam abhūd indīvare mudrite
vyālīnaṃ kalakaṇṭha-manda-raṇitaṃ mandânilair manditam
niṣpanda-stabakā ca campaka-latā sâbhūd na jāne tataḥ

No ornaments adorn
the glowing moon.
Stars are scattered
through the sky.
Love's bow is frozen now,
and the dark lotus
sealed away.
The cuckoo's moans
have melted to a gentle stillness,
the mild breathing of the breeze.
The *campaka* vine with its round clusters
has ceased its rhythmic swaying, and
beyond all this there is nothing
I can know.

Now Kālidāsa sang:

svinnaṃ maṇḍalam aindavaṃ vilulitaṃ srag-bhāra-naddhaṃ tamaḥ
prāg eva prathamāna-kaitaka-śikhā-līlāyitaṃ susmitaṃ
śāntaṃ kuṇḍala-tāṇḍavaṃ kuvalaya-dvandvaṃ tiro-mīlitaṃ
vītaṃ vidruma-śīt-kṛtaṃ nahi tato jāne kim āsīd iti

Sweat drips from the lunar orb.
Blackness, burdened with flowers,
has gone wild.
But just a moment before, a smile unfolded
like dazzling *kaitaka* blossoms,
opening in play.
The dance of the earrings
is now at rest.
Two blue lilies
are half-hidden.
The coral no longer
cries out in ecstasy,
and as for me
and what happened next—
I just don't know.

Bhoja at once declared that Kālidāsa's verse was incomparable—the poet had no equal. (The playful *kaitaka* smile is the clinching evidence in this verdict.) But Bhavabhūti protested, so Kālidāsa suggested that they record the verses on palm leaves, which would be floated in the water of a pot in the temple of Sarasvatī, goddess of poetry.

In the course of this trial, Bhavabhūti's poem floated a little more lightly upon the water than Kālidāsa's weighty verse. The goddess then intervened by adding a grain of pollen, taken on her fingernail from the flower she wears in her ear, to Bhavabhūti's palm leaf. Now the two leaves floated equally on the water, and Kālidāsa said:

aho me saubhāgyaṃ mama ca bhavabhūteś ca bhaṇitaṃ
ghaṭāyām āropya pratiphalati tasyāṃ laghimani
girāṃ devī sadyaś śruti-kalita-kahlāra-kalikā-
madhūlī-mādhuryaṃ kṣipati paripūrtyai bhagavatī

Lucky me! When both our statements
were balanced on the water,
something seemed a little lacking

until the Goddess of Words
threw in the sweetness
of a single grain of pollen
from the white blossom
in her ear

and there was fullness
everywhere.

Both verses are built around conventional metaphoric identifications: the full moon = the face of the beloved; the nocturnal sky = her hair; the Love God's bow = her eyebrows; the blue lilies = her dark eyes; the cuckoo's cries = the gasps and moans of love; the *campaka* vine = her body, and the *campaka* clusters = her breasts; coral = her lips. See *Bhojaprabandha* 251–53 and the discussion in the After-Essay.

Love and Marriage

What woman would dare
to blame me? Aren't you a woman yourself?
Don't you know how to make a man
fall in love? Did I call him
while he was in *your* arms?
Did I break into your house
and drag him, kicking and screaming,
to me?

e vanital mamun dalapan emi pano tamar āḍuvāru gā-
ro valapiñcu nerp'ĕrugaro tama ḵaugiṭilonan uṇḍagā
rāv' adiy emirā vijayarāghavay añc' ilu dūri balmimai
tīvaraḵattĕnai vĕliḵi tīsuḵa vaccitinā talodarī

Attributed to Raṅgājamma, a learned courtesan poet in the court of Vijayarāghavanāyaka at Tanjavur (mid–seventeenth century). The queen sent a maidservant with a painted picture of the king to Raṅgājamma, to beg the courtesan to return her husband to her (*pati-bhikṣa*). Raṅgājamma scribbled this verse on the back of the painting and sent it back to the queen.

A Definition of Myth

They say you saved an elephant—
but it's not true.
And that story about your giving Draupadī endless saris
is a lie.
That you saved a crow with a gracious glance—
that never happened.
And when they say you gave a kingdom to the brother of your
  enemy—
that's simply fiction.

Still, Kṛṣṇa, son of Devakī,
it could *all* be true
if you would just
take care of me
today.

ḳari gācindi huḷaḳḳi
draupadiḳi ḳoḳal mĕcci iccindi dabbara
ḳāḳâsurunin ḳaṭâḳṣamuna raḳṣiñcind' abaddhamb' aho
śaraṇ annan pagavāni tammuniḳi rājyamb' iccuṭal ḳalla
ittari nan gāccina niḳḳam' ī ḳathalu
ḳṛṣṇā devaḳī-nandanā

Kṛṣṇa/Viṣṇu is said to have saved the elephant Gajêndra from a crocodile; to have given Draupadī an unending string of saris when Duḥśāsana tried to disrobe her publicly, in the Kuru court; as Rāma, to have saved the life of a crow-demon (at the cost of one of the crow's eyes); and, again as Rāma, to have given Rāvaṇa's kingdom to the demon's brother, Vibhīṣaṇa.

Similes

Her face is like the moon.
(Just so.)
To drink her lips is like sipping
Essence of Eternity.
(Indeed.)

But grabbing her hair in a frenzy to kiss her with fire and delight:

what's *that* like?

candra-sadṛśaṃ mukham asyāḥ
amṛta-sadṛkṣaś ca mukha-rasas tasyāḥ
sa-kaca-graha-rabhasôjjvala-
cumbakaṃ kasya sadṛśaṃ tasyāḥ

Included in some editions of *Sarasvatī-kaṇṭhâbharaṇa* of Bhoja.

Three in One

A courtesan speaks:

That whiff of jasmine, that's my daughter
just outside my door.
Look at her.
But *I'm* the expert in the arts of love—
look at me.
And that young girl,
eyes unfolding like a lotus—
she's my daughter's daughter.
Look at her.

Now tell me what you choose to be—
son-in-law,
husband,
or grandson
to me!

mŏlla sugandhi kūtur'adi mungiṭan unnadi dāni jūḍu nen-
ĕlla vidhambulan ratulan elĕḍu dānanu nannu jūḍum
utphulla-saroja-netra-vara-putrika putrika dāni jūḍu nāk'
alluḍav' ayyĕdo magaḍav' ayyĕdavŏ manumanḍav' ayyĕdo

The customer replies:

That whiff of jasmine just outside the door—
I won't say no to her.
You're the expert in the arts of love.
I won't say no to you.
And that young girl,
eyes unfolding like a lotus,
your daughter's daughter,
I won't say no to her.

So let me be
son-in-law,
husband,
and grandson
to you.

mŏlla sugandhi k̲ūturini muṅgiṭa ganṭini dāni mānan' īv
ĕlla vidhambulan ratulan elĕḍu dānavu ninnu mānan' ut-
phulla-saroja-netra-vara-putrik̲a putrik̲a dāni māna nīk̲'
alluḍan' ayyĕdan magaḍan' ayyĕda nī manumanḍan' ayyĕdan

Ravished?

She comes down sickened
off the soft bed,
hands tugging at her wild hair,
both eyes glowing red.
Tremors ripple through her waist, her face
is turned away.
She holds her sari
with her fingers, for the knot
has come undone,

as she staggers slightly
through the needle of light
from the diamond lamp
high on its stand
into the shadows below.

The great poet Pĕddana began this poem:

mṛdu-talpambu vik̲āra-līla ḍigi dhammilambu cebūni rā-
ga-da-drg-jālamutoḍa k̲aunu nuliyūgan momu mārvĕṭṭucun
vadalam bārina nīvi paṭṭuk̲ŏniy ā vāmâk̲ṣi aṭl' egĕ—

Here Pĕddana became stuck, unable to finish the verse, but his daughter then produced the following concluding line (reproduced in the English above after the stanza break):

tat-
sadana-bhrājita-ratna-dīpa-k̲aḷik̲ā-sthambhambu k̲rīnīḍak̲un

A Small Request

Yesterday I saw that lovely woman
in the field of maize.
Since then—no sleep.
Please, Lord of Springtime,
bring her and me together.
I'll bring you flowers.

jŏnna cenu kāḍa
sŏgasukattĕnu cūci
ninnaṭelaniñci nidara ledu
dānni nannu gūrci dayajūḍu mādhavā
pŏnna-pūlu tĕcci pūja setu

Anonymous and composed in low-caste dialect but perfect meter.

Love Letter

Dear X,

Your tiny waist (almost not there),
your grace, the gentle
way you walk—
I bless all these, for they
are yours.
Hoping you're well.
I'm well enough.
Please send me news,
good news,
since every moment
I want you more,

Sincerely yours,

śrīmad-asatya-madhyamaku cinni vayāriki muddulāḍikin
sāmaja-yānakun migula cakkani intiki melu gāvalen
mem' iṭa kṣemam' īvaraku mī śubha-vārtalu vrāsi pampumī
nā madi nīdu mohamu kṣaṇambunu tīradu sneha-bāndhavī

Ascribed to Śrīnātha.

Tops

One day a courtesan embraced the famous poet Kūcimañci Timmakavi in the middle of the street; embarrassed, Timmakavi turned away his face. She then asked him:

"You're the best of all my lovers, which is why
I hugged you. You think it's fair
to turn your face away?
I thought you had good taste!"

caturulalona nīvu ḳaḍu jāṇav' aṭañcunu biṭṭu ḳaugiliñ-
citin' iṭu māru mom' iḍaga jĕllune o rasiḳâgragaṇya

Timmakavi replied:

"Not at all, my dear.
I was just trying to see
if those two breasts of yours,
spinning like tops made of gold,
had shot straight through my chest
and come out behind me."

adbhutam' agu raṅgu baṅgarapu bŏṅgarapun gava bolu
  nī ḳuca-
dvitayamu rŏmmu nāṭi ala vīpuna dūsĕn' aṭañcu cūcitin

Ungiving

My eyes look away in shame.
My hand shrinks back.
My mouth—normally quite mobile—
just won't open.
It's all a waste.
Even my bones seem aflame

when a woman serves food
without love.

kāṇakkaṇ kūcute kaiyĕṭukka nāṇute
māṇŏkka vāytiṟakka māṭṭāte—vīṇukk'ĕṉa
ĕṉp' ĕllam paṟṟiy ĕrikiṉṟat' aiyaiyo
aṉp'illāḷ iṭṭav amutu

Ascribed to Auvaiyār.

Minor Joy

Ampikāpati, the son of the great poet Kampaṉ, fell in love with the daughter of the Choḻa king and sang her beauty in his verse. Her father, the king, was enraged and wished to execute the young poet but, at the advice of the latter's teacher, Ōṭṭakkūttar, instead gave him a chance to redeem himself by singing publicly a hundred verses on the subject of "real joy," that is, the experience of the divine (*periṉpam*). If, however, even one of the verses were to relate to "minor," that is, erotic, joy (*ciṟṟ'iṉpam*), the poet would be killed. Ampikāpati then sang an invocatory verse followed by ninety-nine verses on God. The Choḻa princess, mistaking the invocatory verse for one of the set, erroneously concluded that her lover had passed the trial; she rose from her seat to congratulate him. At this point Ampikāpati, overcome, let a verse in praise of her beauty slip through his lips—the final, hundredth verse. The angry king now condemned him to death. To his heartbroken father, Kampaṉ, who was unable to understand how this fatal "slip" had happened, Ampikāpati offered the following proud explanation:

Speak of courage? Who has courage
when the Love God's arrows strike?

As for time, there's no more time
once a lover has looked
straight at you.

No point in trying to strike a bargain
when your heart is already lost.

You can't damp the fire of passion
with soggy words.

Is love wrong?

vīram uṇṭo maṯaṉ kaiyampiṉāl vĕntu vīḻukaikku
neram uṇṭo vañci nerpaṭṭa kālaiyil nĕñcai viṭap
peram uṇṭo cŏllav oṇṇāta kāmap pĕrunĕrupukk'
īram uṇṭov aiyaṉey ĕṉṉa pāvam iṉic cŏlvate

Fate

After the execution of Ampikāpati, his father, Kampaṉ, mourned him in the following verse:

Bound by the fantasy of fusing
with women gentle as a doe,
breasts flowing honey,

what love have you ever known?
Though you fell prey to the arrows
of mad Desire, still I'd hoped your heart
might reach toward clarity.

Now you are gone, my son,
cut down by Man's
first fate.

maṭṭuppaṭāk kŏṅkai māṉār kalavi mayakkattile
kaṭṭuppaṭṭāy ĕṉṉa kātalpĕṟṟāy mataṉ kaiyampiṉāl
paṭṭuppaṭṭāyiṉum teṟuvaiyey ĕṉṟu pārtt'irunteṉ
vĕṭṭuppaṭṭāy makaṉe talai nāḷiṉ vitippaṭiye

White Light

All of Mayilai, great Tiruvāli's home,
is washed in white
when the salt-seller walks its streets

    with lakes and coral,
    bows and arrows,
    embedded in her face,
    flooding moonlight
    in her smile.

aṇṇaṟiru vāliy aṇimayilai attaṉaiyum
vĕṇṇilaviṉ coti virittate—naṇṇum
taṭantuppu viṟpāṇan taṉmuk̲atte kŏṇṭu
naṭant' uppu viṟpāḷ nak̲ai

Attributed to Kampaṉ. When the goldsmith Tiruvāli asked the poet for a verse to immortalize him, Kampaṉ glanced out into the street and sang this stanza. A woman's forehead is conventionally compared to a wide lake, her lips to coral, her eyebrows to a bow, and her glances to arrows; smiles in India are always white.

Progress

At first, we were two,
with a single body
between us.
Later, we became "lovers."
Today, we are husband and wife.
Kind sir, can you tell us
what further misery lies in store?

muṉṉāḷ iruvarkkum yākkaiy oṉṟāka muyaṅkiṉamāl
piṉṉāṭ piriyaṉ piriyaiy ĕṉṟāyiṉam pecaluṟum
iṉṉāṭ kŏḻunaṉ manaiviy ĕṉṟāyiṉam iṉṉamumor
ciṉṉāḷil ĕppaṭiyov aiya nīyiṉṟu cĕppukave

Ascribed to Antakakkavi (Vīrarākava Mutaliyār). This is a Tamil version of a well-known Sanskrit stanza from the Amaru collection *Amaruśatakam*, ed. Vedam Veṅkaṭarāya Śāstri (Madras: 1950), no. 81:

purâbhūd asmākaṃ prathamam avibhinnā tanur iyam
tato nu tvaṃ preyān vayam api hatâśāḥ priyatamāḥ
idānīṃ nāthas tvam vayam api kalatraṃ kim aparam
hatānāṃ prāṇānāṃ kuliśa-kaṭhinānāṃ phalam idam

The great nineteenth-century singer, Makāvaittiyanātaiyar, sang this (Tamil) verse at the end of a concert in the presence of a former patron who no longer showed any interest in his music. The poem achieved the desired effect: the patron had a change of heart.

First Words

The world is really two, made of name and form.
One the poet creates.
The second comes from God.

nāma-rūpâtmakaṃ viśvaṃ dṛśyate yad idaṃ dvidhā
tatrâdyasya kavir vedhā dvitīyasya caturmukhaḥ

Cited by Vĕmparāla Sūryanārāyaṇa Śāstri, commentary to Piṅgaḷi Sūranna, *Prabhāvatī-pradyumnamu* (Vijayavada: Veṅkaṭrāma Grantha Māla, 1962), 1.

What's Wrong?

"Is he a good lover?"
"He's great."
"Is he inventive in bed?"
"Full of ideas."
"Handsome?"
"He beats the god of love himself."
"But does he love you?"
"Like no other."
"If that is so, why are you running around
with other men?"
"You're bold, you're experienced,
you ought to know about these things.
There's only one thing wrong with him:
he happens to be
my husband."

sarasuḍu k̲āḍŏ jāṇa rati-sampada ledŏ samṛddhi rūpamo
maruni jayiñcu moham' asamānamĕ inniyu k̲algi jāravai
tirigĕdav' ela bāla ati-dhīravu prauḍhavu nīv' ĕruṅgave
nĕra gṛhamedhiy an paluk̲u nīcamu tocĕ k̲ŏrant' ade sumī

Attributed to Śrīnātha.

How Not to Be a Fool

Don't eat while you're walking, or laugh while you're talking.
Don't worry about the past, or regret what was done.
When two are together, never
be the third.

khādan na gacchāmi hasan na jalpe
gataṃ na śocāmi kṛtaṃ na manye
dvābhyāṃ tṛtīyo na bhavāmi rājan
kiṃ kāraṇaṃ bhoja bhavāmi mūrkhaḥ

Too Shy

"Why are you staring at the floor, young lady?
Did you drop something there?"
"You idiot, can't you see?
This jewel of a moment
has slipped away."

adhaḥ paśyasi kim bāle tava kiṃ patitaṃ bhuvi
re re mūḍha na jānāsi gataṃ tāruṇya-mauktikam

Samayôcitapadyamālikā, 21.

Bedtime Story

When a courtesan asked the poet-client to tell her a story, he replied:

Now is the time.
The Moon has set out on his course.
The south wind rouses and arouses,
the cuckoo calls at every watch.

If we survive,
if we're still here,
still able to use human words
after the violence of loving
clears, then
and only then
I'll tell you a tale.

comaṉ puṟappaṭat tĕṉṟalum vīcat tuyilŏḻiya
yāmaṅka ṭoṟuṅ kuyilvantu kūvuman nerattile
nāmum* piḻaittu manitarmuṉ peciṭa nāmumuṇṭāyk
kāmak kalakkan tĕḷintapiṉ nāṉuṅ kataicŏlvaṉe

Ascribed to Kāḷamekappulavar.

*v.l. *nāvum*: "if we still have a tongue."

Freedom

Final freedom is that state of no pain,
no pleasure, no qualities, nothing—
or so some idiot has said.

But when a ravishing young woman,
drunk on desire,
is free from her clothes—
that's freedom
for me.

avidita-sukha-dukhaṃ nirguṇaṃ vastu kiṃ cid
jaḍa-matir iha kaś cin mokśa ity ācacakṣe
mama tu matam anaṅga-smera-tāruṇya-ghūrṇan-
mada-kala-madirâkṣī-nīvi-mokṣo hi mokṣaḥ

Do It

Day by day, we're getting old.
Fuck me now, and as long as you can.
Who will give you, when you're dead,
with the rice-and-sesame balls
a clean-shaven cunt?

dine dine gacchati nātha yauvanam
yabhasva nityaṃ yadi śaktir asti ced
mṛtasya ko dāsyati piṇḍa-sannidhau
tilodakaiḥ sārdham alomaśaṃ bhagam

Funeral offerings include balls of rice and sesame as food for the dead.

Nameless

You know why the ring finger has no name in Sanskrit?
Once they tried to count the poets,
bending the little finger first, for Kālidāsa.
Then there was no one
even close.

purā kavīnāṃ gaṇanā-prasaṅge
kaniṣṭhikâdhiṣṭhita-kālidāsā
atrâpi tat-tulya-kaver abhāvād
anāmikā sârthavatī babhūva

The ring finger is called *anāmikā*, "nameless," in Sanskrit. When counting on one's fingers in India, one begins with the pinky.

It Never Rains but It Pours

The boss is coming for dinner.
The maid dropped dead.
The car is totaled.
It's raining hard.
The mortgage payment is overdue.
My ear aches.
Workmen are drilling in front of my house.
My new wife is in labor.
My first son is getting married.
My son-in-law is upset because he wants more.
The computer is down.
I'm broke,
and it's New Year's Eve.

I must be having
a bad day.

guruvula rāka dāsi mṛti gurrapu dāṭulu vānay ĕjjaḍin
pŏruguna appu bādha cĕvi poṭunu muṅgiṭa dŏmmarāṭayun
marusati garbhavedana kumāru vivāhamu allun' alkayun
karuvu daridram' ābdikamu kalgun' ŏk'appuḍĕ kṛṣṇabhūvarā

We have slightly modernized the original Telugu contexts.

The Real Reason

Śiva sleeps on Mount Kailāsa.
The sun and the moon live in the sky.
Vishṇu rests on a snake.

Anything to avoid bedbugs.

śivuḍ' adrini śayaniñcuṭa
ravi-candrulu minṭan unṭa rājīvâkṣunḍ'
aviraḷamuga śeṣunipai
pavaḷiñcuṭa nalli bādha paḍaleka sumī

A Sanskrit version exists:

kamale kamalā śete
haraś śete himâlaye
kṣīrâbdhau ca hariś śete
manye matkuṇa-śaṅkayā

We thank Ashok Aklujkar for this verse.

Won't Wash

Viṣṇu, fortunately, can afford silk.
Śiva has taken to wearing leather,
and Bhairava, completely frustrated,
has given up clothes altogether—
anything to avoid the hassle
of the washerman.

cāk̲ivanitoḍa jagaḍālu paḍalek̲a
siragalāḍu paṭṭu cīra gaṭṭĕ
śivuḍu tolu gaṭṭĕ chīy ani madi rosi
bhairavunḍu cīra pāravaicĕ

Washermen notoriously give excuses for failing to do their job—there is no water today, it is raining—and are also said to wear their customers' clothes themselves or to rent them out. Bhairava is Śiva's naked form.

A Poet's Thirst

Śrīnātha, tormented by thirst in the dry Palnadu region, addressed Lord Śiva with the following ironic request for a drink of pure river water:

A rich god like Kṛṣṇa can marry
thousands of women.
For a beggar like you, even two is too many.
Śiva, let me have Gaṅgā.
Pārvatī is enough for you.

sirigalavāniki cĕllunu
taruṇula padiyāruvela taga pĕṇḍl'āḍan
tiripĕmunak' iddar'āṇḍlā
parameśā gaṅga viḍuvu pārvati cālun

Gaṅgā is the river Ganges, Śiva's second wife, held in his matted locks. Śiva is famous for his form as Bhikṣāṭana-mūrti, the wandering beggar.

Critic's Choice

The beauties of a poem are best known
by the critic.
What does the author know?
The beauties of a woman are known
only to her husband.
What does a father know?

ḳavitā-ḳanyaḳa-guṇamulu
ḳaviḳanna rasajñuḍ' ĕrugu ḳavi em' ĕrugun
bhuvilo ḳanyaḳa-guṇamulu
dhavuḍ' ĕrugunu gāḳa ḳanna taṇḍṛ' em' ĕrugun

In a Word

Words make the gods give an answer.
Words make kings give you gifts.
For words, women give you pleasure.
You are lost, and humbled,
without words.

māṭalaceta devatalu mannana cesi varambul' iccĕdar
māṭalaceta bhūpatulu mannana cesi dhanambul' iccĕdar
māṭalaceta ḳāminilu mannana cesi suḳhambul' iccĕdar
māṭalu nervaḳ'unna avamānamu nyūnamu māna-bhaṅgamun

Measure for Measure

There's as much bread as there is dough,
as much pride as there is power.
A pound is no heavier than the weighing-stone.
A whore gives no more than she gets.

piṇḍ' ĕntŏ rŏṭṭiy 'ante
maṇḍalapati manuv' adĕntŏ mānuṣam' ante
guṇḍ' ĕntŏ tūnik̨' ante
miṇḍani īv' ĕntŏ lañja meḷamul' ante

We thank Arudra for remembering this verse.

It's the Job

You're a drop of water on a lotus leaf.
Poets compare you to a pearl, but that's no reason to be proud.
You're praised because of your position.
Could a woman wear you on her necklace?
Could you be given as a gift?

sthānaviśeṣa-mātramuna tāmarap'ākuna nīṭi bŏṭṭa nin-
pūnika mauktikamb' anucu polcina mātrana garvam' eṭikin
mānavatī-śiromaṇula mauktikam' anduna kūrpa vattuvo
kānukal' īya vattuvŏ vikāsamu tĕttuvŏ melu tĕttuvo

Another *anyâpadeśa* verse, addressing undeserving people in high office.

Whatever It Takes

Break a pot.
Tear your clothes.
Bray like a donkey,
if you have to.
Somehow or other,
become famous.

ghaṭaṃ bhittvā paṭaṃ chittvā kuryād vā gardabha-svanam
yena kenâpy upāyena prasiddhaḥ puruṣo bhava

A Poet's Opinion

When Bhavabhūti completed his great drama, the *Uttara-rāma-carita*, he sent someone to recite it to Kālidāsa. The latter listened while engaged in a game of chess. When Bhavabhūti asked what the great poet's response was, the servant said, "Nothing." "He said nothing at all, the whole time?" asked Bhavabhūti. "Well, at one point, his maid gave him betel nut together with lime (Telugu *sunnam*); he chewed a bit and said, 'There's a touch too much lime.'" *Sunna* means a nasal consonant: from this, Bhavabhūti immediately saw that his poem had one nasal too many.

The following verse, describing Rāma and Sītā's happy nights in their forest exile, exists in two variants, differing only in the extra nasal in the final line:

Whispering wonderful whatevers
in any which order,
cheek touching cheek,
arms totally enmeshed
from so much loving

we never knew the hours' passing
when suddenly night itself was over—

kim api kim api mandam mandam āsakti-yogād
aviralita-kapolaṃ jalpator akrameṇa
aśithila-parirambha-vyāpṛtâikâika-doṣṇor
avidita-gata-yāmā rātrir eva vyaraṃsīt

The second variant, obviously inferior, reads:

rātrir evaṃ vyaraṃsīt

We never knew the hours' passing:
That's how the night was spent.

See discussion of this story in the After-Essay.

What the World Needs

Who needs a basketful of glittering stones?
One true blue sapphire will suffice.
In this world, one good poem
will do.

nikkam'aina indra nīlam' ŏkkaṭi cālu
taḷuku bĕḷuku rāḷḷu taṭṭĕḍ' ela
cāṭu-padyam' ŏkaṭi cāladā bhuvilona
viśvadâbhirāma vinura vema

Attributed to Vemana, the author of a *śataka* of gnomic verses.

Don't Bank on It

Not even God can save the money
you have when you are rich
for the moment you might need it.

If you pour light
from the full moon
into a safe, can you take it out
on a moonless night?

kalanāṭi dhanamul' akkara-
galanāṭiki dāca kamala-garbhuni vaśamā
nĕla naḍimi nāṭi vĕnnĕla
alavaḍune gādĕ boya amavasa-niśikin

This verse is attributed to Allasāni Pĕddana. The clown-poet Tĕnāli Rāma, hearing the unusual final phrase of Pĕddana's verse—*amavasa-nisi*, instead of *amāvāsya-niśi*, i.e., a shortened and collapsed form with no consonant clusters or long vowels—parodied the verse with the following lines, artificially depleted of all the usual clusters and long vowels:

ĕmi tini sĕpitivi kapitamu?
bamapaḍi vĕri puccakāya vaḍi tini sĕpito?
umĕtaḥ-kaya tini sĕpito?
amavasa-niśi anina māṭa alasani pĕdanā?

We thank Pillalamarri Ramakrishna for remembering this verse.

What did you have for breakfast,
Alasani Pĕdana,
before you made this verse?
Probably the squash
that makes poetry
into mush.

The exaggerated, ridiculous effect of the dropped consonants and vowels can hardly be reproduced in translation. Note, however, that even the poet's name, Allasāni Pĕddana, has been comically reduced.

The Unlucky Eight

One: travel to an alien land.
Two: cooking for yourself.
Three: deserting your beloved wife.
Four: begging for a living.
Five: depending on your peers.
Six: working for someone who doesn't appreciate you.
Seven: having to speak before scholars when your mind is
blank.
Eight, and last: real poverty.

These are the eight calamities,
O Lord on the Kaveri's shore.
Who needs them?

araya paradeśa-yātra ceyuṭay oṇḍu
tanaku tāne vaṇḍu-kŏnuṭa rĕṇḍu
kula-satin' ĕḍa-bāsi tŏlagi-povuṭa mūḍu
vĕlayaṅga yācaka-vṛtti nālgu
tana sarivari pañcanu ceru-koṇṭ' aidu
gurut' ĕruṅgani rāju gŏlucuṭ' āru
caduvu nerakay uṇḍi sabhaku povuṭa eḍu
ĕnna dāridryambun' ĕnmidavadi

aṣṭa-kaṣṭambul' aniyĕḍun avvi ivvi
kāna iṭuvaṇṭiv' ĕvvarik'aina valadu
cārutara-mūrti devatā-cakravarti
ramya-guṇa-dhāma kāveṭi raṅgadhāma

The First Rule

If it happens, it happens.
If it doesn't, it doesn't.
If you try to force it to happen,
you're left with an arrow in your heart.

āḵumpot' āḵum aṉaittum atuv ŏḻintu
poḵumpot' ĕllāmum poḵume—veḵa
navacarampaṭṭāṟ pol nalintu matanĕñce
avacarampaṭṭāl āḵumā

Anonymous. *Taṉippāṭal tiraṭṭu*, ed. Karuppakkiḷar Cu. A. Irāmacāmippulavar (Madras: SISS, 1972), 5:252.

Bitter-Sweet

The Tree of Life is bitter,
but it has two sweet fruits:
good poetry
and a good friend.

saṃsāra-viṣa-vṛkṣasya dve phale amṛtôpame
kāvyâmṛta-rasâsvādaḥ saṅgatiḥ saj-janaiḥ saha

What's the Difference

People with no taste for good poetry
are no different from cattle,
though they don't chew grass.
Lucky for the cows.

sarasa-ḵavita ruciy ĕrugani
puruṣula paśuvul' ani nikḵamugan ĕruguḍu vār'-
uruvaḍi tṛṇambu meyami
pariḵimpaga dharaṇi paśula bhāgyamb' ĕndun

Maḍiki Siṅganna, *Saḵala-nīti-sammatamu* 31.

An Ode to the Nose

In agony, the *campaka* blossom wondered
why bees enjoy the honey of so many flowers
but never come to her.
She fled to the forest to do penance.
As a reward, she achieved the shape of a woman's nose.
Now she takes in the perfumes
of all the flowers, and on both sides
she is honored by eyes
black as bees.

nānā-sūna-vitāna-vāsanalan ānandiñcu sāraṅgam' e-
lā nann' ŏllad' aṭañcu gandhaphali bal kānan tapamb' andi yo-
ṣā-nāsâkṛti dālci sarva-sumanas-saurabhya-samvāsiy ai
pūnĕn prekṣaṇa-mālikā-madhukarī-puñjambul ir-vaṅkalan

Poets often compare a woman's nose to the *campaka* flower and her eyes to bees. Indian folklore insists that bees never come near this flower or its vine. The verse, ascribed to Nandi Timmana (known ever after as Mukku Timmana, "Timmana of the nose"), explains the prehistory of these associations. The poet Bhaṭṭumūrtti is said to have purchased this verse from Mukku Timmana and to have included it in his great poem, *Vasucaritra*. One of the beauties of the Telugu original is the preponderance of nasal sounds.

Who's Stopping Them?

The bee is drawn to all the blossoms
as he moves through the forest.
The only one he never touches
is the virginal *campaka* vine.
Is she not lovely?
Couldn't he love her
were God not standing in the way?

caran vanânte nava-mañjarīṣu na ṣaṭ-pado gandha-phalīm ajighrat
sā kiṃ na ramyā sa ca kiṃ na rantā balīyasī kevalam īśvarâjñā

Attributed to a poetess-princess named Tukka. For another use of the convention of bees and the *campaka* vine, see the previous poem. Tukka is said to have composed five cryptic love poems, all built around tragic images of the bee and the flowers. Here is the story told about these poems:

> Kṛṣṇadevarāya's father, Narasā-Nāyaka, was told by a passing Brahmin to sleep with his (Narasa's) wife at a certain auspicious hour in order to beget a son. (Some say that a star fell from heaven into the king's water pot while he was bathing. He covered the pot and con-

sulted with his minister Timmarasu, who told him to drink the water and sleep that same night with his wife.) The queen, who was summoned to come, spent too long dressing and adorning herself, so Narasā-Nāyaka slept instead with a maidservant who came to light the lamps. Kṛṣṇadevarāya was born from this union and thus became known as a *dāsī-putra*, son of a maidservant. This made it extremely difficult for him to marry. Eventually, Timmarasu arranged a match with Tukka, the daughter of the Gajapati king of Vinukonda—although the women of the household were against marrying the princess to this man of mixed birth and determined to kill the prospective bridegroom. Kṛṣṇadevarāya insisted on seeing the bride before the wedding, so he came to Vinukonda disguised as the servant who carries betel, in the retinue of Timmarasu. But he had forgotten to take off the emerald-studded anklet on his foot, and the princess recognized him by this sign; so she fled back to the women's quarters and informed everyone that the despicable bridegroom had arrived. The women rushed out to kill him, but Timmarasu spirited him out of the palace and the fort.

The wedding was performed in the absence of the bridegroom, who was represented, as was customary in royal households, by a sword. The bride, dressed by her maidservants with swords hidden around her waist, was then sent to her husband at Vijayanagara, the imperial capital. She was, in fact, reluctant to take part in the scheme to kill the king. When Kṛṣṇadevarāya approached his new wife in the bedroom, the swords fell from her side. At this, on Timmarasu's advice, the princess was sent back to her father's house. Tukka was ashamed to return home in this way and decided to remain, instead, at a place called Kambham in Rayalasima, in the vicinity of two hills, which she connected by building a mud bank to hold water. There, in a mode of regret and longing for the husband she had been sent to kill, she composed these verses.

See Gurujāḍa Śrīrāmamūrti, *Kavi-jīvitamulu* (1893; 5th ed., Madras: Vāvilla Rāmasvāmiśāstrulu and Sons, 1955), 477–80, 546–54. For a somewhat different version of the story, see Uṭukūri Lakṣmīkāntamma, *Āndhra-kavayitrulu*, 2d ed. (Secunderabad: published by author, 1980), 33–35.

Real Kinship

Stronger, even, than the bond
that comes from having the same mother
are the bonds we make
by sharing words.

ŏk̲k̲atalli k̲'ŏppan udayambu bŏndina
bāndhavambuk̲aṇṭe bahuguṇamula
vasudhan' ĕnni cūḍa vāg-jāta-bāndhavamb'-
adhik̲am'anḍru cūvey āryul' ĕlla

Maḍiki Siṅganna, *Sak̲ala-nīti-sammatamu* 744.

I was born for poetry.
Making good poems is my business.
That's how I'll cross to the other shore.
All my fortune comes from poetry.
I've conquered death, and I'll defeat old age.

If anyone faults my poetry, even my teacher,
even God himself, I'll fight back
and win.

k̲avanārthamb 'udayiñcitin su-k̲avitā-k̲āryambĕ nā-vṛttiy ī-
bhavam' addāna tarintu tad-bhavama mad-bhāgyambu sarvambu mṛt-
yuvu ne dāna jayiñcitin ruja jayintun dānicen aṭṭi nā-
k̲avanambun guruḍ' emi lĕk̲k̲a haruḍe k̲āḍ' āḍa vāḍ' āḍĕdan

Composed c. 1930 by Cĕllapilla Veṅkaṭa Śāstri, the last great improviser of Telugu verse, when his teacher, Śrīpāda Kṛṣṇamūrti Śāstri, found flaws in his poems. Printed in Cĕllappilla Veṅkaṭa Śāstri, *Jayanti* (published by poet, 1937), 41.

After-Essay

1. SYSTEMIC CRITICISM AND METAPOETIC STATEMENTS

The poems we have translated belong to a large corpus, whose major features we outlined in the Introduction. Before we explore the intricacies of this poetic world, let us restate its contours. *Cāṭu* verses, in the sense we have defined—not simply any isolated individual stanza but also remembered verses in popular, oral circulation—form part of an internally coherent system, which seems to have emerged at a particular historical moment in south India. Once an existing poem (for instance, from a classical source) enters this system, it is transformed in highly specific ways; poems created within the *cāṭu* tradition naturally embody its particular understanding of poetry, the poet's role and power, and a metaphysics of language proper to this system. The mode of transmission and elaboration is entirely oral; once *cāṭus* are collected and recorded in manuscripts or printed books, they belong to a different stage of literary history and mean something different. Usually *cāṭu* verses are ascribed to highly visible poets and associated with narratives about them. Ascriptions of this sort often constitute a peculiar form of commentary or criticism in their own right: a *cāṭu* attributed to Śrīnātha is, almost ipso facto, certainly not to be seen as composed by the historical Śrīnātha; rather, it will be a verse composed after the manner or in the style of Śrīnātha, and as such it will illustrate and comment upon that style or upon Śrīnātha's image and his characteristic themes. The tradition knows its classical texts so well that it can come up with new verses amazingly akin to the "originals"; but this process is, in general, a kind of *displacement through identification*, which allows for incisive commentary upon or criticism of the great poets' works through innovative imitation. (It is also, of course, possible for Śrīnātha to compose a *cāṭu* verse in the style of Śrīnātha.)[1] Similarly with patrons: verses praising a given donor (*birudu-gadyas*, for example, which list the patron's titles and honors) are *not cāṭus* unless they become integrated into the whole *cāṭu* system, in which case their import changes radically. The image of the patron becomes inflated to an enormous degree, and the poet's image also fits the *cāṭu* milieu. The system as a whole is pervaded by very powerful notions which, taken together, comprise a mode of literary criticism no less insightful than the more formalized and self-conscious tradition of Sanskrit poet-

1. One thinks of the story of Mayakovsky, who once brought some new poems of his to R. Jakobson. After a few days, Mayakovsky asked his friend how he liked these poems. "They are very good," said Jakobson, "but not as good as Mayakovsky."

ics, the *alaṅkāra-śāstra*. Indeed, we would be tempted to argue that the *cāṭu* form of criticism and literary theory is the most subtle and penetrating ever produced in southern India; certainly, it is the critical mode most closely engaged with, and suited to, the works of the Tamil and Telugu classical traditions from which it has drawn its major voices. These works are linked by the *cāṭu* tradition into a coherent ecosystem of types and tastes, densely intertextual, and "framed" by the critical stance implicit in the process of selection.

In this sense, the deepest cultural expressivity of the system is profoundly rooted in the interconnectedness it posits and unfolds—never in the superficial isolation of a given verse. Each *cāṭu* echoes others and contributes something to the consistent articulation of the system as a whole. Let us try to see how this works in practice.

The medieval Sanskrit tradition assembles all its greatest poets at the court of King Bhoja, where they compete with one another in performing great feats of improvisation, memory, and near-omniscient knowledge. Sometimes the king himself sets a theme for the poets and then judges the results. Thus one day Bhoja asked Kālidāsa and his rival Bhavabhūti—remember that all historical or chronological incongruities are collapsed in the *cāṭu* milieu—to improvise verses on the subject of *ratyanta*, "the end of love," that is, the moment immediately following upon orgasm. Here is Bhavabhūti's verse:

muktābhūṣaṇam indu-bimbam ajani vyākīrṇa-tāraṃ nabhaḥ
smāraṃ cāpam apeta-cāpalam abhūd indīvare mudrite
vyālīnaṃ kalakaṇṭha-manda-raṇitaṃ mandânilair manditam
niṣpanda-stabakā ca campaka-latā sâbhūd na jāne tataḥ

No ornaments adorn
the glowing moon.
Stars are scattered
through the sky.
Love's bow is frozen now,
and the dark lotus
sealed away.
The cuckoo's moans
have melted to a gentle stillness,
the mild breathing of the breeze.
The *campaka* vine with its round clusters
has ceased its rhythmic swaying, and
beyond all this there is nothing
I can know.

Kālidāsa's verse was rather different:

svinnaṃ maṇḍalam aindavaṃ vilulitaṃ srag-bhāra-naddhaṃ tamaḥ
prāg eva prathamāna-kaitaka-śikhā-līlāyitaṃ susmitam
śāntaṃ kuṇḍala-tāṇḍavaṃ kuvalaya-dvandvaṃ tiro-mīlitam
vītaṃ vidruma-śīt-kṛtaṃ nahi tato jāne kim āsīd iti

Sweat drips from the full moon.
Blackness, burdened with flowers,
has gone wild.
But just a moment before, a smile unfolded
like dazzling *kaitaka* blossoms,
opening in play.
The dance of the earrings
is now at rest.
Two blue lilies
are half-hidden.

The coral no longer
cries out in ecstasy,
and as for me
and what happened next—
I just don't know.

In some ways these verses are strikingly similar: each is built around conventional metaphoric identifications (the face of the beloved = the full moon, her eyes = two dark lotuses, her mouth = red coral, her long black hair = the night sky, and so on), and each ends with a suggestion of open-ended infinity or fullness, couched as "unknowing" ("beyond all this there is nothing I can know"). These final statements are, however, formulated slightly differently, and not by chance. Indeed, perhaps the most striking feature of the poems, seen together, is the way each of them simulates to perfection the style, syntax, diction, and poetic organization of each of the two poets respectively. Bhavabhūti's verse is a smooth configuration of discrete nominal sentence units, each with its finite verb; one thus has the impression of brief verbal flashes that start and quickly finish and also cumulate and intensify in effect toward the middle of the third line, with its resonant alliteration and repetition—*kala-kaṇṭha-manda-raṇitaṃ mandânilair manditam*, "The cuckoo's moans / have melted to a gentle stillness, / the mild breathing of the breeze." *Manda*—"gentle," "mild," "slow"—describes both the cuckoo's moaning and the breeze, and then recurs unexpectedly, but in a manner altogether characteristic of Bhavabhūti, in a denominative verb, *manditam*. The breeze thus breathes mildly and gently against the muffled drumming of these repeated background syllables. Still more striking is the poet's stance at this delicate moment of transition: Bhavabhūti speaks in images that infuse the entire cosmos with the feeling and perception of stillness produced out of passionate movement and the wholeness of love.

Kālidāsa's verse is patterned in a very different manner. Here the nominal sentences seem to flow together in a liquid movement that rapidly issues into the extraordinary compound of the second line: *prathamāna-kaitaka-śikhā-līlāyitam* [*susmitam*], "[a smile unfolded] like dazzling *kaitaka* blossoms, / opening in play." The current races forward, and the poem is still alive with motion; perhaps Kālidāsa is describing a moment just prior to that of Bhavabhūti's verse. And if Bhavabhūti's imagery tends toward the cosmic range, Kālidāsa's seems almost surrealistic: "Blackness, burdened with flowers, / has gone wild"; "The coral no longer cries out in ecstasy." The metaphoric identifications have somehow autonomized themselves, as if the consciousness that produced them had been swept away or transcended by the energies released in the course of loving. Moreover, Kālidāsa's depiction is consistently humanized and also concretized: we hear of real sweat, and real earrings, and above all a real smile. This last element, the dazzling smile of the beloved, is entirely missing from Bhavabhūti's poem; and perhaps for this reason, and also because of the striking compound that articulates the smile, King Bhoja is said to have declared at once that Kālidāsa was the superior poet. Indeed, so the *Bhoja-prabandha* tells us in this context, the king insisted that a poet who could invent a phrase like *prathamāna-kaitaka-śikhā-līlāyitam* was not even properly human, but rather a divine being playing at earthly existence.

And yet the tradition that gives us these two stories is not content with this judgment. The story continues: Bhavabhūti was not prepared to accept defeat, so Kālidāsa suggested they put the verses to an empirical test. Each poet would write his poem on a palm leaf, and the two leaves would be floated in a pot of water in the temple of Sarasvatī, Goddess of Arts; the more substantial and weighty verse would sink a little more deeply in the water. When this trial was carried out, Kālidāsa's verse at first sank a little more into the water than Bhavabhūti's. But now the goddess intervened, unwilling to let Bhavabhūti be defeated—he was, after all, a great poet. With her fingernail she flicked a tiny grain of pollen from the flower she wore in her ear onto Bhavabhūti's palm leaf. Now the two verses floated at an equal level, and Kālidāsa sang the following poem:

aho me saubhāgyaṃ mama ca bhavabhuteś ca bhaṇitam
ghaṭāyām āropya pratiphalati tasyāṃ laghimani
girāṃ devī sadyaś śruti-kalita-kahlāra-kalikā-
madhūlī-mādhuryaṃ kṣipati paripūrtyai bhagavatī

Lucky me! When both our statements
were balanced on the water,
something seemed a little lacking

until the Goddess threw in the sweetness
of a single grain of pollen
from the white blossom
in her ear

and there was fullness
everywhere.

What was lacking? Was it that joyful, intimate smile of the living woman? Or some slight failing in Bhavabhūti's construction? Kālidāsa's second poem has something ambiguous in it; it is not clear if this is a generous statement on the part of a great poet who can easily afford to be generous, or rather an elegant reassertion of his own triumph over his rival. In any case, one should notice the way the tradition focuses, in this third verse, on the latent issue of fullness (*paripūrti*). *Ratyanta*, the "end of love," like Vedânta, the "end of metaphysics," appears in the guise of completeness, satiety, and an awareness transformed to a point where there is no longer room for knowledge or for words. Yet this total experience of fullness is, in effect, problematized by the *cāṭu* narrative frame, which produces the graphic image of a trial and then requires a minute but still critical intervention by the goddess before the physical experience of wholeness can become fully present in the poems. It is, perhaps, a matter of a single grain of pollen, no more than that—but also no less. The same concern with totality, or rather with the near miss that leaves room for the goddess, is now, by implication, referred back to the original description of love. The *cāṭu* poems have the courage to face the ever-so-human reality of the always slightly incomplete.

We may remark in passing that this conceptualization of ultimacy, achieved through poetic process, differs starkly from the aesthetic goal presented by the Sanskrit poeticians of the *dhvani* school, who speak of *brahmâsvāda*, "tasting God," as the final, perfect (if transient) achievement of literary or dramatic art. This *brahmâsvāda*, or *brahmânanda*, is still differentiated from, say, the yogi's stable transformation in ontic state: the aesthetic tasting of ultimacy is *brahmânanda-sabrahmacārin*, a "schoolmate" or an approximation of the real metaphysical end. Still, what the *cāṭu* poet seeks is of another order, a perfection that exists within language, one that can be translated from words into world, and that is always concretized in taste and feeling, has weight and texture—like a drop of pollen, or like two palm leaves floating in water—and is also clearly subject to minute or momentary lapses and failures, to greater or lesser realization, and to a range of experienced forms. Stated schematically, the difference lies partly in the contrast between an idealized and abstract emotion, the goal of the great Sanskrit poeticians such as Abhinavagupta, and the concrete, physically felt experience that the *cāṭus* celebrate. *Rasa*, the "taste" or "feeling" of the *dhvani* scholiasts, now becomes, in the *cāṭu* world, an actual fluid.[2] *Mādhurya*, the abstract quality of syllabic mellifluousness, becomes a substance, for example, a woman's lips. Even the beauty of a poem itself can be quantified by its weight when recorded on a palm leaf. Moreover, each of these qualities or notions is entirely capable of being stated in language without resorting to a statement of supralinguistic ineffability.

In most cases, the kind of juxtaposition and commentary we see in this story offers remarkably trenchant observations about the great figures of the tradition. Let us look at another example, again linking Kālidāsa and Bhavabhūti, but this time with reference to a famous verse from an existing text—Bhavabhūti's great drama, the *Uttara-rāma-carita*. In the first act of this play we find a verse in which Rāma, the hero, recalls nostalgically the delightful nights he and his beloved wife Sītā spent in the forest during their exile—*before* Rāvaṇa kidnapped Sītā and hid her away in Laṅkā. Here is the verse:

2. See p. 53.

kim api kim api mandaṃ mandam āsakti-yogād
aviralita-kapolaṃ jalpator akrameṇa
aśithila-parirambha-vyāpṛtâikâika-doṣṇor
avidita-gata-yāmā rātrir eva vyaraṃsīt

Whispering wonderful whatevers
in any which order,
cheek touching cheek,
arms totally enmeshed
from so much loving,

we never knew the hours passing

when suddenly night itself was over.

There is, however, a variant reading for the final line:

rātrir evaṃ vyaraṃsīt

That's how the night was spent.

So much for the textual evidence; the only difference in the two lines lies in the nasal *m* of *evam*, "thus," as opposed to the emphatic *eva*. Now let us see what the *cāṭu* tradition has done with this variation. They say that when Bhavabhūti had completed his play, he sent a servant to recite it in the presence of Kālidāsa; Bhavabhūti had some doubts, and wanted the great poet's approval. Kālidāsa listened to the recitation while engaged in a game of chess. At some point he sent his servant to bring him some betel nut, coated with lime (*sunnam* in Telugu), which he chewed happily while playing and listening to the poem. Afterward, the servant returned to Bhavabhūti, who asked if the master had said anything about his work. "Nothing at all," said the servant. "Truly nothing? Did he utter anything at all?" cried Bhavabhūti, dismayed. "Well," said the servant, "he did say that there was a little too much lime (*sunnam*) on the betel." Now one needs to know that *sunna* in Telugu also means a nasal consonant; so Kālidāsa's comment could be taken to mean that the *Uttara-rāma-carita* was perfect except for one extra nasal—that is, the *m* of *evam* in the variant reading of the line quoted above. Indeed, there is no doubt at all that *eva* is a superior reading, and that the line is better in the form we cited first. Bhavabhūti recognized this as well and removed the troubling *m* from his text. Notice that Kālidāsa's comment is offered indirectly—that is to say, delicately and ambiguously—but at the same time in a form linked, again, to entirely concrete, sensual experience, the taste of betel with a little too much lime. Connoisseurs of betel chewing will know that every ingredient must be perfectly balanced to produce the requisite bodily feeling; if there is too little lime, the chemical reaction fails; if there is too much, the mouth may blister. The same kind of balance is necessary in savoring a poem.

Sometimes the tradition allows the poet himself to comment on his own works. A story about Kampaṉ tells us that the poet left the Choḻa country in anger, after an argument with his patron, the king. In disguise, he wandered from court to court until he arrived in the Cera land, where he assumed the role of a servant offering betel to the Cera king. Hidden in this manner, one day he heard the king's poets and pandits discussing two verses from his own *Rāmāyaṇa*. Although their explications were subtle and ingenious, they fell far short of Kampaṉ's own intention; and eventually the lowly betel carrier found a way to explain publicly, to the court, the true, underlying richness of the two poems.[3] Notice that the poet is allowed to explain himself, to unfold the manifold meanings of his work, only when in disguise—though eventually the goddess of poetry, Sarasvatī, reveals his identity to the Cera king, who then assumes the lowly role of betel carrier he had previously allocated to the great poet.

There is a certain poignancy to this vision of the poet, moved by divine forces, capable of turning language to his own creative purposes in the world—yet at the same time trapped in exile and disguise, or even afflicted by yet more severe forms of personal suffering that become reflected in his work. A famous Tamil story about Kampaṉ describes the poet's loss of his son, Ampikāpati, executed by the Choḻa king after the boy fell in love with the Choḻa princess.[4] After this, the tradition says, Kampaṉ composed his *Rāmāyaṇa*, one of the masterpieces of Tamil literature. But the *Rāmāyaṇa* tale also has its bereaved father—Daśaratha, who died of grief when his son Rāma left for the forest. Kampaṉ sang this story, which echoed his own loss; and, so the *cāṭu* tradition tells us, at one point in the process of composition the poet also sang the following verse, ostensibly about Rāma, but really about himself:

parapp'ota ñālam ŏrutampiy āḷap paṉimatiyam
turappoṉ ŏrutampi piṉvarat tāṉum tuṇaiviyuṭaṉ
varappona maintaṟkut tātai pŏṟātuyar māyntaṉaṉ nĕñ-
curappov ĕṉakk' iṅk' iṉiyār uvamai uraippataṟke

One brother [Bharata] remained behind to rule the wide world.
Another brother [Lakṣmaṇa], brilliant as moonlight,

3. Vīracāmi Cĕṭṭiyār, *Vinota-raca-mañcari* (Madras, 1876), 132–35.
4. See pp. 98–100.

followed Rāma and his wife to the forest.
The father could not bear the grief of losing
his son, so he died.
Only I, with my heart of stone, survive
to tell the tale.

Kampaṉ, the poet as witness, empathically identified with his heroes, defines the anguish of the storyteller kept alive by the need to tell his tragic story.

This verse shows us yet another major side to the *cāṭu* tradition—the side that is fascinated with metapoetic issues that focus on the nature of poetic and linguistic creativity. An astounding number of *cāṭus* deal explicitly with these themes. The reader will encounter them throughout our collection, and we will shortly turn to a closer examination of the specifically linguistic problems; but to illustrate the trend, we may cite the following verses:

nāma-rūpâtmakaṃ viśvaṃ dṛśyate yad idaṃ dvidhā
tatrâdyasya kavir vedhā dvitīyasya caturmukhaḥ

The world is really two, made of name and form.
One the poet creates.
The second comes from God.

Clearly, in some sense the poet comes first, before the creator god himself. "Reality" is molded by the poet's voice. But this power over language takes specific forms, involving a play with indirection and the subtle twists characteristic of poetic speech, as the *cāṭu* tradition tells us:

ghanatara-ghūrjari-kuca-yuga-kriya gūḍhamu gāka drāviḍī-
stana-gati teṭa gāka aracāṭ 'agu āndhra-vadhūṭi cŏkkapun

canu-gava-līla gūḍhatayu cāṭutanambunu leḳay uṇḍa cĕp-
pinan adipo ḳavitvam' anipiñcu nagiñc' aṭugāḳay uṇḍinan

Not entirely hidden,
like the enormous breasts of those Gujarati women,
and not open to view,
like a Tamil woman's breasts,
but rather,
like the supple, half-uncovered breasts
of a Telugu girl,
neither concealed nor exposed:

that's how a poem should be composed.
Anything else is a joke.

Not by chance, of course, the Telugu *cāṭu* makes its point, and clarifies the internal hierarchy in poetry, by an analogy with Telugu women. By far the most extended metapoetic statement of this type—a tour de force involving a contrast between Sanskrit and Telugu poetic textures—is the *Utpalamāliḳa* verse attributed to Pĕddana (see pages 34–36), which also marks a historic point of transition in the evolution of the classical tradition.[5]

2. CREATIVE TAUTOLOGY: THE MAGIC OF LANGUAGE

We have seen that the *cāṭu* poet has the power to change reality by words. We can understand this power in various ways and in varying intensities. In some sense, this type of poet is paradig-

5. See V. Narayana Rao, *Tĕlugulo ḳavitā-viplavāla svarūpam* (Vijayavada: Viśālândhra Pracuraṇālayam, 1978).

matic for all "real" forms of speech.[6] Cursing and blessing inhere in language; the poet is one who is capable of actualizing, often in a literal manner, this insistent potential. There are, however, somewhat less dramatic exemplifications of this theory—moments when the poet gently and playfully teases reality to conform to his purpose rather than harnessing the world to his highly charged words. Behind these moments lies a complex and intriguing theory of linguistic modes. Let us begin with a slight, though charming, example:

vara-bimbâdharamun payodharamulun vak̰râlak̰ambul mano-
hara-lolâk̰ṣulu cūpak̰' avvali mŏgamb' ainantan em' āyĕ? nī
guru-bhāsvaj-jaghanambu k̰rŏmmuḍiyu māk̰un cālave? gaṅgak̰' ad-
dari mel' iddari k̰īḍunun galadĕ? udyad-rāja-bimbânanā

Full red lips, breasts, curls,
darting eyes that steal the heart:
so what if you show me
none of these, what if
you turn the other way?
Can't I make do
with your curved and ravishing behind
and your coiled braid?
Is there merit on one side of the river
and no fun on the other side
when the full moon flashes in water
like your smile?

6. As Mandelstam is said to have remarked about the Symbolists: "Symbolism is redundant, since every true use of language is an incantation."

The trickster poet, Tĕnāli Rāmaliṅgaḍu is addressing a woman who has turned away from him in bed. He begins with standard features of feminine beauty seen from the front—lips, breasts, curls, eyes—and then renounces them in favor of the "curved and ravishing behind," which is all he can see. This in itself is, no doubt, a pleasant compliment to the sulking beloved, but the poet perseveres. Both banks of the Ganges have their merits; it is all one river, pictured now, by implication, at moon-rise, the time of erotic rendezvous. The metaphor speaks for itself—speaks, we can assume, to the woman's recalcitrant mood. But the real turning point comes only in the final syllables of the verse, which are a vocative addressed to the woman "whose face is like the rising full moon" (*udyad-rāja-bimbânanā*). This is a description of her smile, the culmination of the entire portrait, and we can be certain that it works. No Telugu woman attuned to poetry could resist this address; so one must imagine the beloved turning back to her poet-suitor with a radiant smile. Another way to describe the process is to speak of a perceived lack or blockage which is initially compensated by poetic devices, then removed or turned around.[7] The conclusion of the verse belies its opening statement, which insists that the woman's back is good enough; the final vocative rolls the poem over and presents us with a smiling face. This movement within the poem is surely followed, one must assume, by a parallel one outside it.

As already stated, this is a simple example of a process that is, more generally, part of the *cāṭu* poet's normal effect upon his world. He speaks, and reality assumes the form he has pro-

7. We wish to thank Dina Stein for this formulation.

duced in language: a subtle vocative can effect this transformation no less than an entire, dramatic verse. The pattern we have just witnessed is an ancient one, attested in Tamil from the Cankam poems of the early centuries A.D., as in the following example from the *Kuruntŏkai* anthology (spoken by the heroine's female companion):

nīrvār kaṇṇai nīyiva ṇŏḻiya
yāro pirikiṟ pavare cāraṟ
cilamp'aṇi kŏṇṭa valañcuri marā attu
veṉi lañciṉai kamaḻum
temū rŏnnuta ṉiṉṉŏṭuñ cĕlave

You're crying now, but you won't
be left behind. Could anyone
take himself away from you,

your forehead sweet as the fragrance
of the whorled white *kadamba* blossoms
flowering in spring on the mountain slopes?

If he goes, he'll go
with you.[8]

As the modern editor U. Ve. Cāminātaiyar notes in his commentary on this poem, the extended vocative that forms its center also reproduces its external movement: the heroine is languishing in sorrow because her lover has disappeared; her girlfriend comforts her, assuring her that no man could bring himself to leave her. She addresses the heroine: literally, "You whose forehead is sweet as the fragrance of the whorled, white

8. *Kuruntŏkai* 22, by Ceramāṉ ĕntai. See note by U. Ve. Cāminātaiyar, in his edition of the text (2d printing, Madras: Kapīr Press, 1947), 58.

kadamba flowers. . . ." Already in the course of this long phrase, the heroine, comforted by her friend's initial reassurance, brightens and smiles: her brow assumes the radiance and fragrance that the simile suggests. In effect, the poem has produced this transformation by its verbal magic; the explicit conclusion is almost redundant, a restatement of the opening in the context of the change that has taken place in the heroine's awareness.

The *Kuṟuntŏkai* verse nicely exemplifies the level of continuity in technique, and in underlying presuppositions, from the most ancient strata of south Indian poetry through the medieval *cāṭus*. There is more that could be said of this line of development; in many ways, the *cāṭu* milieu preserves, and also extends, typological features of the poet and his craft that were obscured in the classical Sanskritic *alaṅkāra* tradition. The *cāṭu* poet has something of the Vedic *ṛṣi*, manipulating or generating concrete experience through the largely internal mechanisms of poetic vision and speech, as we shall see. But these mechanisms have a characteristic flavor and direction in the *cāṭu* verses, which also sometimes show the marks of the scholastic *alaṅkāra* analyses, tropes, and techniques. Let us look closely at a disarmingly simple example from Tamil, which turns out to be surprisingly eloquent in terms of an implicit metaphysics of language.

This famous stanza was supposedly improvised serially by Kampaṉ and the poetess Auvaiyār in the following manner. An impoverished courtesan named Cilampi wanted Kampaṉ to compose a verse for her. Since his minimum fee for a stanza was a thousand gold coins, she sold or mortgaged all her possessions, but still only achieved the sum of 500 coins. She offered this payment to the poet, and Kampaṉ, stubbornly holding to his standard, took the money, wrote only *half* a stanza on the wall of Cilampi's house, and went away. Here is Kampaṉ's beginning to the verse:

taṇṇīrum ḵāviriye tārventaṉ colaṉe
maṇṇāva tuñcoḻa maṇṭalame—

The Kāviri
is water.
Our Choḻa lord
is the king.
The Choḻa land
is all earth—

Now silence—a break and blockage. Poor Cilampi was devastated by this failure, until one day the aged Auvaiyār came by and read the unfinished verse. In exchange for a bowl of gruel, she completed it as follows:

—pĕṇṇāvāḷ
ampŏṟ cilampi aravintat tāḷaṇiyum
cĕmpŏṟ cilampe cilampu

Cilampi
is a woman,
and on her foot, soft as a flower,
the bright gold anklet
is an anklet.

Cilampi, enriched by this verse, also became wealthy in other ways: her anklets at once turned to gold. In this way the poetess is said to have received one of her epithets, *ḵūḻuḵḵuppāṭi*, "the Woman who Sang for a Bowl of Gruel." Paradoxically, the poetess who was content with a bowl of gruel produces riches for Cilampi, whereas the expensive court poet Kampaṉ renders her destitute. Here Kampaṉ is the prototype of the mercenary poet who makes a living by selling his syllables, while Auvaiyār is more the saint who has the divine gift of conferring blessings out of compassion, expecting almost nothing in return.[9]

Formally, nothing could be simpler than the syntax of this poem, which consists of a series of five nominal equation-sentences—although the final two of the series can be seen as linked in a genitive hypotaxis. As is not uncommon in Tamil sentences of this type, in the first equations the predicate precedes the subject:

taṇṇīrum	=	*ḳāviriye*
water	=	Kāviri
[predicate + conjunctive]		[subject + emphatic]

The third and fourth items preface and replace, respectively, the emphatic particle *e* with emphatic derivatives of the verb *āḳu*, "to be," thus slightly expanding the equation.[10]

It all looks, and is meant to look, somewhat trivial. For this the poet could claim 500 gold coins? Is it surprising to be told that the Kāviri flows with water, or that the king looks like a king? In any case, Kampaṉ's half of the verse is an axiomatic series, reinforcing the obvious identities: A = A, and B = B.

Does Auvaiyār's half redeem the situation? Clearly, judging by the story, it must: Cilampi is transformed through the poet-

9. There is a parallel in Telugu to the roles of Śrīnātha, the classical court poet, and Potana, supposedly his brother-in-law, the devotional poet, when these two figures are set in opposition.

10. Literally, the Tamil characterizes Cilampi, too, as golden (*cĕm pŏṟ-*), that is, radiant or beautiful, like the gold of the anklet (*am pŏr-*). "Gold," we might say, effectively rhymes with "gold."

ess's words. But this transformation reflects the change from a purely axiomatic series to a creative act which forces the axiom into existence. The Kāviri is, no doubt, water; but Cilampi's anklet is not gold until the poetess speaks of it as such. There is a shift between the two halves of this verse: the first part merely sets the stage for the magic of the second. Kampaṉ's equations may be poetical, but Auvaiyār's are ripe with a deeper potential. In this particular context, she is the real *cāṭu* poet. Her means are, however, still embedded in the syntax and texture of her poem. Notice how she immediately makes present the living named woman Cilampi in the escalating series of identifications. Even more striking is the fact that this name is no accidental concatenation of syllables but is rather meaningfully linked to a golden promise: *Cilampi* resonates with *cilampu*, anklet. Indeed, the great charm of this little verse lies in the culminating triple repetition of these syllables:

ampŏṟ CILAMPI aravintat tāḷaṇiyum
cĕmpŏṟ CILAMPE CILAMPU

And here, too, the repetition has an internal, ascending logic. The nominal equations have miraculously moved to a point where subject and predicate truly coincide. The anklet is an anklet—just that (or rather: *cilampu* is *cilampu*). No space intervenes between the "object," to use a term already deeply misleading, and the verbal token that constitutes or "creates" it. This is undoubtedly the highest point reached in the progressive series, and it is just this moment of total self-coincidence that makes the poem so moving and effective. This is the point where the true transformation—base metal to gold—takes place.

Syntactically, the sign—and perhaps the actual instrument—of this transformation is the shift of the emphatic *e* from subject to predicate. All of the first axiomatic equations put this emphasis on the subject: *taṇṇīrum kāviriye*, "The Kāviri / is water." In the Tamil, predicate precedes subject, and it is the latter that is marked. But Auvaiyār highlights, by this single emphatic syllable, the predicate, thus reversing the pattern: *cĕmpŏṟ cilampe cilampu*, "the bright gold anklet / [is] an *anklet.*" The golden object does not yet exist: it comes into being precisely through the poet's subtle device, which forces the coincidence of name and being. Stated differently, the poetess inserts into the series of equational sentences a further identity statement, *not* originally part of the series, but now an integral part—because she says so.

Such complete coincidence within language and experience is both rare in the extreme and inherently paradoxical, like most identity statements. We have, then, in this slight stanza, come a long way from the initial declarations of axiomatic equivalence. To make matters still more surprising, it turns out that this "existential" coincidence of the word-thing with itself is also somehow implicit in this woman's name, and hence in her "fate." No wonder she becomes enriched. "Magic" here means the unlikely ability of something to be itself, and to coincide with its name. Perhaps only the poetess can see this identification, or hear the latent resonance of the name; certainly it is the poetess who has the ability to externalize this resonance in her poem, thereby forcing the future into the open, as it were. Auvaiyār, that is, uses words to turn a surface reality into gold.

A successful poet, in the world of the medieval *cāṭu*, is always capable of such effects. He or she is akin to a magician, whose props are the *mantra*-like words that he or she commands. Indeed, the resonances of a word like *mantra* are very relevant here, for, as we have said, these medieval poets have acquired something of the Vedic *ṛṣi*'s peculiar power to work upon reality. A long history issues into these images of the poet's role: the *ṛṣi* sang from a place of heightened consciousness, and his words were enigmatic and obscure; the epic *muni*, by way of contrast, spoke (rather than sang) with the clarity of omniscience, and his words were heavily and primarily referential in tone; the medieval *kavi* sings, again in a strange and complicated mixture of enigmatic meaning and simple reference, and in a manner that makes his utterance effective in the world, as blessing or curse. Missing from this rudimentary typology is the classical court poet, who sings ornate and polished works produced out of premeditated and calculated intentionality—works which may well reduce external realities to the status of pale and impaired replicas or fragments of the poet's world-creating vision, with its assumed perfection. In general, however, this latter type—the erudite and accomplished court poet—is assimilated in the *cāṭu* narrative tradition to the image of the wandering, improvising, magically potent *kavi*.

A powerful and contrastive metaphysics of language informs this series. At stake are both the expressivity of human language as such and the transformative and creative potential hidden in poetic utterance. We could spell out some of these issues by means of another traditional classification. Veda or *mantra* are, we are told, *śabda-pradhāna*, that is, the constituent sounds predominate (over sense and meaning). *Śāstra* ("science") is *artha-pradhāna*, focused on meaning (rather than sound). *Kāvya* is *śabdârtha-pradhāna*: the aesthetic, or phono-aesthetic, dimension is equal in weight to the dimension of meaning. Real poetry, that is, in the eyes of the poeticians, can never divorce content from form. Neither aspect can be touched or tampered with without at once affecting the other.

But the world of the medieval *cāṭu* offers yet another division, as becomes clear from our examination of the composite Kampaṉ-Auvaiyār verse. There is something here of the *mantra*, which changes both awareness and external experience, as well as something of *kāvya*, which substitutes one (internal) reality for another by means of irreplaceable and compelling combinations of syllables and words. The peculiar configuration of meaning is, however, of a different order entirely and allows for, indeed, depends on, denotative reference. The surface structure is deceptively simple, whereas underneath is a complex statement about correspondence and identity, or about movement toward an ontic tautology of word and object. In this struggle within language, and between language and the world, all forms of displacement—especially what we would call metaphor—are decisively discounted, like half-paid-for half-poems.

One might point to further ironies. For all their bitter differences over the locus and extent of convention (*saṅketa*) in language, both the grammarians and the Mīmāṃsakas agree that naming (*saṃjñā*) belongs in this domain; indeed, there is a temptation to think of naming as a particularly reduced and perhaps even arbitrary or adventitious (*yadṛcchā*) instance of convention.[11] The *cāṭu*'s veiled assertion of an ontic tautology of the name—which we could relate to the underlying iconicity of poetic language generally—cuts right across the predominant Sanskrit theory in this domain. This is no small achievement in

11. See discussion by Mammaṭa, *Kāvyaprakāśa* 2.2.

its own right. It also implies a certain scorn for the Sanskrit poeticians' penchant for labeling and classifying. To cite one deft and typical example, from Bhoja's *Sarasvatī-kaṇṭhābharaṇa*:

candra-sadṛśaṃ mukham asyāḥ
amṛta-sadṛkṣaś ca mukha-rasas tasyāḥ
sa-kaca-graha-rabhasojjvala-
cumbakaṃ kasya sadṛśaṃ tasyāḥ

Her face is like the moon.
(Just so.)
To drink her lips is like sipping
Essence of Eternity.
(Indeed.)

But grabbing her hair in a frenzy to kiss her with fire and delight—
what's *that* like?[12]

The poet reserves all his energy for the final long compound that confronts us with an experience entirely resistant to labeling or comparison. Only the poet can somehow contain it; at the same time metaphor and simile, as abstract notions, are utterly demolished.

3. *PARA-PŪRITA* VERSES: VOICES ACROSS THE GAP

The verse just discussed, like others cited in the Introduction, belongs to a large class of *cāṭus* attributed to more than one author. In many cases, these multiple-voiced *cāṭus* reflect a situation of improvisation and contest, as when the king or patron

12. Ironically, Bhoja cites this verse as an example of *lupta-upamā*, with the explicit word of comparison hidden by the *samāsa*.

offers one line of a verse and demands that his court-poets complete the rest. This is known as *samasyā-pūraṇa*—filling out a riddle-like text. Sometimes a single poet, like Kālidāsa, can complete the entire verse; but in other cases, one has poems composed, sequentially, by a committee. For example: King Bhoja sang the following line as *samasyā* for his poets:

carama-giri-nitambe candra-bimbaṃ lalambe

[as] the Moon rests his head in the lap of the Western sky.

This is a description of dawn, and Bhoja's line is the projected fourth out of four. The first is contributed by the eloquent Bhavabhūti, given to feats of hypnotic assonance:

aruṇa-kiraṇa-jālair antarikṣe gatarkṣe

In the red glow of morning, stars fade from heaven.

Daṇḍin sings the second line:

calati śisira-vāte manda-mandaṃ prabhāte

A cooling breeze moves through the dawn like a sigh.

It remains for Kālidāsa to complete the verse with the third, penultimate line:

yuvati-jana-kadambe nātha-muktoṣṭha-bimbe

Lovers leave one last kiss on the lips of young women.

Each of the lines is true to the style of the poet to whom the story attributes it; but Kālidāsa, of course, is the one who manages to humanize the description, thereby giving life and dynamism to the poem and stimulating the listener's feeling—a somewhat technical and predictable evocation of the dawn has suddenly become pregnant with the sweet sorrow of separation after a night of love. Note that although Bhoja's line technically completes the verse, it is really Kālidāsa who makes it into a finished poem, which now reads:

In the red glow of morning, stars fade from heaven.
A cooling breeze moves through the dawn like a sigh.
Lovers leave one last kiss on the lips of young women
as the Moon rests his head in the lap of the Western sky.

More common, however, are those verses that have only two voices, usually interwoven in dialogue; and the dominant pattern is one which insists that the first "author" becomes stuck, unable to continue the verse, and has to be rescued, as it were, by an intervention from outside, in the form of another poetic voice (sometimes that of the god). The *cāṭu* tradition has its own poignant manner of epitomizing this pattern: Nannaya, the first Telugu poet and the author of the first parts of the Telugu *Mahābhārata*, died before completing the *Vana-parvan*, the third book of the epic. The last verse he sang is a description of night in the forest:

śārada-rātrul' ujjvala-lasattara-tāraka-hāra-paṅktulan
jārutarambul' ayyĕ vikasan-nava-kairava-gandha-bandhurô-
dāra-samīra-saurabhamu dālci sudhāmśu-vikīryamāṇa-kar-
pūra-parāga-pāṇḍu-ruci-pūramulan paripūritambulai

Autumn nights under the glowing canopy of stars—
dense with the wind-borne fragrance
of unfolding water lilies,
flooded with light white as camphor
flowing down from the moon.[13]

13. Nannaya 3.4.1422.

But there is an alternate, and better, reading for the concluding line—°*pūramul' ambara-pūritambulai*:

> flooded with light white as camphor
> flowing down from the moon,
> and filled with sky.

The *cāṭu* tradition naturally prefers (and perhaps even created) this latter reading, which also allows for a pregnant pun: dividing the words differently, we get °*para-pūritambulai*, "completed by others." This, says the tradition, is evidence that Nannaya knew that this verse was his last, and that his work would be completed by others. Language itself embeds this perception, ambiguously coded, in the alternative readings of an autumnal verse: the poet tells us, as he tells himself, that at this point his work will be truncated, and a silent space opened up—like the sky-filled nights in the forest. Or rather, it is the oral tradition of the *cāṭus* that, once again, lifts a verse out of its classical text and uses it to draw an image of the poet at the very moment his voice is silenced, at the point of proleptic transition toward the distinct cadences of other, later voices.

We have taken the tradition's own term—*para-pūrita*, "completed by others"—to refer to this complex and central pattern in the *cāṭu* corpus. One poet sings, and stops; another resumes, usually in a manner that coincides with, or indeed generates, the external concretization of the poem's visionary reality. Between the two voices there is a creative, and tension-filled, space—and it is in this space that the poem, and often the world, are transformed. The discontinuity allows movement, and often the elevation or intensification of the poetic voice, which may also work its magic outside the verse. Ampikāpati, in love with a Chola princess, sings two lines ecstatically praising her beauty when she appears before him in court:

*iṭṭ'aṭi novav ĕṭutt'aṭi kŏppaḷikka
vaṭṭil cumantu maruṅk'acaiya—*

Too delicate to touch the ground,
her foot blisters as she walks,
her body swaying under the weight
she carries—

Kampan, the poet's father, seeking desperately to hide his son's infatuation from the king, turns the verse into a description of a young, low-caste woman selling tubers in the street outside.

*—kŏṭṭik
kiḻaṅko kiḻaṅk' ĕṉṟu kuṟuvāṇāvil
vaḻaṅk' ocai vaiyam pĕṟum*

—as she calls, "Buy my tubers,
sweet tubers for sale,"
in a voice that melts the world.

The king rushes to the window to see if there is anyone in the street; Sarasvatī, goddess of poetry, assumes the form of just such a woman, a basket of tubers on her head, to suit the poet's description.[14] Together, son and father have made a poem with a slight sting—the transition from princess to the low-caste girl who is a goddess in disguise.

There are more complicated and suggestive examples. Potana, author of the Telugu *Bhāvagata-purāṇa*, was composing the poignant section describing Lord Viṣṇu at the moment his devotee Gajêndra—the elephant caught in the fangs of a croco-

---

14. *Taṉippāṭaṟ-ṟiraṭṭu*, 168.

dile—cried to the god for help. Potana wrote the first two words of a verse ("There, in heaven . . . ") and stopped; not knowing how to complete the poem, he went out for a walk. Meanwhile, God himself came in Potana's form, sat down in the poet's house, and wrote the remainder of the verse as Potana's young daughter watched. When her father returned and saw the complete poem, he asked her, in amazement, who had written it down. "You wrote it yourself—have you forgotten?" answered the daughter. Potana then knew that God had given him a helping hand—and the Telugu tradition continues to insist that this entire passage of the classic text bears the mark of divine origin.[15]

This story gives a special role to the poet's young daughter, who witnesses the divine act of poesis. There is a somewhat similar, but far more intricate and ambiguous story about the daughter of Pĕddana, the supreme embodiment of the classical Telugu tradition. Pĕddana is said to have composed the opening lines of the following unusual verse, which speaks of a woman coerced into making love:

mṛdu-talpambu vikāra-līla ḍigi dhammilambu cebūni rā-
ga-da-dṛg-jālamutoḍa kaunu nuliyūgan momu mārvĕṭṭucun
vadalam bārina nīvi paṭṭukoniy ā vāmâkṣi aṭl'egĕ—

She comes down sickened
off the soft bed,
hands tugging at her wild hair,
both eyes glowing red.

15. See discussion in D. Shulman, "Remaking a Purāṇa: The Rescue of Gajendra in Potana's Telugu *Mahābhāgavatamu*," in *Purāṇa Perennis*, ed. W. Doniger (Albany: SUNY Press, 1993), 145–46. Similar stories are told of Jayadeva, the author of *Gīta-Govinda*.

Tremors ripple through her waist, her face
is turned away.
She holds her sari
with her fingers, for the knot
has come undone—

At this point the poet came to a halt, unable to complete the verse; his daughter then offered the concluding line:

—tat-
sadana-bhrājita-ratna-dīpa-kaḷikā-stambhambu krīnīḍakun

as she staggers slightly
through the needle of light
from the diamond lamp
high on its stand
into the shadows below.

This remarkable poem could only have been composed by a woman. Probably the only such surviving statement in an otherwise male-dominated world, the verse manages to present a delicate and disturbing situation where language hardly has words to express sexual violence against women. Who is this woman? The poem is silent, other than saying she is a *vāmâkṣī*, a beautiful woman. The entire opening of the poem, the part attributed to Pĕddana, describes a woman in distress: she gets off the bed sickened (*vikāra-līla*), her eyes glowing red with anger and pain; she clearly cannot stay on that bed any longer, and the description of this bed as soft only enhances the sense of disturbance—it belongs to a comfortable, wealthy man and is soft for him, not for her. Each of the following images intensifies the visual evidence of painful experience, and the series ends with the finite verb *aṭl'egĕ*, "she moved/staggered away." But there is one full line left, if the poem is to be complete. Pĕddana has to stop, leaving an unfinished verse. He has begun something that he cannot bring to conclusion. We are left with an empty, gaping hole, an abyss that consumes the imagination of anyone who follows the poet to this point—until Pĕddana's daughter supplies the last line, a devastating and magnanimous compound, *tat-sadana-bhrājita-ratna-dīpa-kaḷikā-stambhambu krīnīḍakun*:

as she staggers slightly
through the needle of light
from the diamond lamp
high on its stand
into the shadows below.

Every word here bears a closer look. The setting is a *sadana*, a palace (something the earlier part of the verse fails to mention). There are *ratna-dīpa*s, diamonds used as lamps, such as only a king could afford, appropriate only to a royal palace (*rāja-gṛhambu-kanṭĕn abhirāmamugān ilu gaṭṭarādu*, "No one should build a house more beautiful than the king's house," says a verse of the *cāṭu* tradition). The violation took place in the very house of the king. To whom could the woman complain? (*kañcĕye cenu mesina kaladĕ dikku*, "When the fence eats the crop, who is there to guard?" says another *cāṭu* verse.) The only place of comfort in the vast palace where the woman can hide without being seen is the shadow, *krīnīḍa*, cast under the lamp stand (*dīpa-kaḷikā-stambha*). But every Telugu mother tells her daughter never to sit under the shadow cast by a lamp, for it is inauspicious and invites bad luck. In the setting of this verse, however—in a world where everything supposedly auspicious turns evil—the only source of protection is the inauspicious shadow. The majesty of the whole compound with it seven-word length, filled with sturdy aspirates, shimmering liquids, and nasals mediated by long vowels, only highlights the helplessness of the woman. The compound is as long, as wide, and as bitterly stable as the palace where the act of violation occurred. The male voice begins, seeks a mode of expression suited to the unhappy moment, and falls silent; the female voice takes over, boldly seizing the shadows as refuge, while articulating this movement in the elevated and powerful crescendo of a Sanskrit compound that dramatically bears down upon the victim in her flight. Here, as in many of these dialogic *cāṭus*, the mere alternation in voice across the dark gap carries with it a strong intimation of inner movement, enabling closure to emerge on a deeper level of experience and awareness.[16] This

---

16. We might compare the following playful and seductive *cāṭu*, which also describes apparently unwelcome sexual advances thrust upon a woman, but in a tone utterly removed from the darker currents of the Pĕddana verse:

> *akkarŏ nīdu vallabhuḍ' ahaṅkṛti cesina ceta viṇṭivā*
> *ĕkkaḍan ĕkkaḍe mariyun ĕvvarin ĕvvari nannĕ nannĕ nīv'*
> *akkaḍik' ela povalayun ampava ampiti kūḍum' aṇṭinā*
> *mrŏkkiti veḍukoṇṭi nanu muṭṭakum' aṇṭin' ik' emi cesĕdan*

"Sister, do you know what your fine husband dared to do?"
"Where, where, with whom, with whom?"
"With me, with me."
"Why did you go there?"
"You sent me, didn't you?"
"I sent you, but did I ask you to sleep with him?"
"I bowed to him, I begged him,
I told him not to touch me.
What else could I do?"

verse ends in blackness and a full, unmitigated expression of stark suffering, with none of the aesthetic distance habitually structured into the classical, *rasa*-dominated poetics. This kind of freedom, boldness, and emotional directness are significant features of the *cāṭu* world.

4. AUTHORITY AND SUBVERSION

The verse attributed to Pĕddana and his daughter also shows, by virtue both of its theme and the manner of articulation, the occasionally subversive tendency of the *cāṭu* milieu and its predilection for the irregular, the contrary, even the outrageous. A strong parodic drive is conspicuous in the corpus, and takes several distinct forms. Indeed, in general, the *cāṭu* system presents us with a strong critique of traditional structures of authority and their representatives—pandits, literary theorists, established texts on the one hand, and the much-needed patrons of the *cāṭu* poets themselves on the other. Even God comes in for caustic attack: the *cāṭu* poet has the self-confidence to challenge the deity, and to defeat him. Here, for example, is the famous logician Udayanâcārya, who responds indignantly when he arrives in Puri and finds the temple of Lord Jagannātha closed:

aiśvarya-mada-matto 'si mām avajñāya vartase
upasthiteṣu bauddheṣu mad-adhīnā tava sthitiḥ

You're so drunk on wealth and power
that you ignore my presence.
Just wait: when the Buddhists come
your whole existence
depends on me.

The great god needs the services of a trained logician to defend himself against the atheist Buddhists; without Udayana, He may not even exist. This is a kind of *nindā-stuti*, "praise-through-blame," one of the preferred *cāṭu* modes—recall Kāḷamekappulavar's ironic poem on Śiva at Tiruvārūr (cited on page 15). In the complex web of relations that links the poet to the god, the former often has the upper hand.

A similar pattern applies to patrons: despite the poet's material dependence on king or zamindar, his power to curse or bless usually gives him or her a decisive edge (as we have seen in the case of Kāḷamekappulavar). The relationship is not always adversarial, though it is often filled with tension, as many stories demonstrate.

> A certain poet stood in the street as King Appa Rao (Apparāya) of Nujividu was passing in his covered palanquin—apparently he wanted to avoid poets who would pester him for gifts. The poet sang aloud:
>
> *vĕlama kulambun'andun' ilu*
> *vĕḷḷaru kāntal' anaṅga vindun' ap-*
> *palukul' abaddham' āyĕ*
>
> We hear that women of the king's family do not
> walk the streets, but that's not true!

The king was quite angry at this scandalous statement, for the women of the royal family were not supposed to be seen in public; he threw open the doors of his palanquin, ready to punish the poet for his rash statement. But the poet continued:

> —*kulapālaka dhīmaṇi apparāya rāṭ-*
> *kalabhamu kīrti-kānta kṛti-kānta mahī-jaya-kānta muvvurun*
> *kala jagam' antayun tirugagā kanugoṇṭimi citram' ĕnnagan*

See for yourself: the ladies Fame, Poetry and Valor,
queens of the great king Apparāya,
wander everywhere
in this world.

Crisis is averted, the insult deftly turned around. (But has not the poet established his claim and his superior power?) The king, amazed at the poet's cleverness, rewarded him lavishly.

Kings were not merely generous; sometimes they also had good taste and the will to promote it. Two poor Brahmins heard that King Bhoja gave money to poets. Not particularly competent in making poetry, they came up with a line of flat but metrically correct verse, with great effort:

bhojanaṃ dehi rājendra ghṛta-sūpa-samanvitam

O king, give us food, with lentils and butter

Unable to finish the verse, they went to Kālidāsa for help; he sang the second (final) line:

māhiṣaṃ ca śarac-candra-candrikā-dhavalaṃ dadhi

and thick curds, white as the flowing light
of the full moon
on an autumn night.

When the king heard the verse, he said: "Never mind the first half, but give a million coins for each syllable of the second part."

The true poet knows his advantage. One *cāṭu* boldly states:

ākula-vṛtti rāghavu-śarāgramun andu tṛṇāgra-lagna-nīr-
ākṛti vārdhiy iṅkuṭa daśāsyuni jampuṭa mithya gāde vāl-

mīkula sĕppakunna kṛta leni nareśvaru vartanambu rat-
nâkara-veṣṭitāvani vinambaḍad' ātaḍu meruv ĕttinan

The ocean dried up
on the tip of Rāma's arrow
like a dew-drop
at the end of a blade of grass.
And Rāma killed the ten-headed demon.
These stories would be lies
if Vālmīki had not written the *Rāmāyaṇa*.
The world circled by oceans
would never know
if a king lifted the cosmic mountain—
if he did not have a poet
to sing of him.

Yet there is, at times, deep bitterness, as when the Tamil poetess Auvaiyār returns empty-handed from a rich patron:

kallāta ŏruvaṉai yāṉ kaṟṟāy ĕṉṟeṉ
kāṭerit tirivaṉai nāṭā ĕṉṟeṉ
pŏllāta ŏruvaṉai nāṉ nallāy ĕṉṟeṉ
por-mukattuk kolaiyay yāṉ puliye ĕṉṟeṉ
mallārum puyam ĕṉṟeṉ tempaṟ ṟolai
vaḻaṅkāta kaiyaṉai yān vaḷḷal ĕṉṟeṉ
illātu cŏnneṉukk' illai ĕṉṟāṉ
yāṉum ĕṉṟan kuṟṟattāl ekiṉṟeṉe

I sang of learning, and there was nothing.
I spoke of culture, and there was nothing.
I said he was good, but he was a nothing.
I called him tiger—that good-for-nothing.

I mentioned his muscles, which were nothing.
I praised his charity, and he gave me—nothing.
It's all my fault: words about nothing
get me nothing.[17]

More common targets, however, are the rigid representatives of established doctrines and conventional taste, especially in the domain of poetics and aesthetics. One day Bhoja saw Kālidāsa, presumably a vegetarian Brahmin, carrying a fish under his arm. The following conversation ensued:

kakṣe kiṃ tava? pustakaṃ. kim udakaṃ? kāvyârtha-sārôdakam.
gandhaḥ kiṃ? nanu rāma-rāvaṇa-mahā-saṅgrāma-raṅgôdbhavaḥ?
pucchaḥ kiṃ? nanu tāla-patra-likhitaṃ? kiṃ pustakaṃ bho kave?
rājan bhūmi-surais ca sevitam idaṃ rāmāyaṇaṃ pustakam.

"What's that thing under your arm?"
"It's a book."
"Why is it dripping?"
"Must be an overflow of poetry juice."
"So why does it stink?"
"Probably the corpses left behind
when Rāma fought Rāvaṇa to the death."
"But it has a tail!"
"It's written on palm leaves, not yet trimmed."

17. This verse (with slight differences) is also attributed to Irāmaccantirak kavirāyar (*Taṉippāṭaṟ-ṟiraṭṭu*, 348).

"So what book is it, honored poet?"
"My lord, it's the one even Brahmins relish,
that fishy tale about God."

Here, as in so many stories, the *cāṭu* poet flouts convention: he has become a fish-eater (elsewhere, a meat-eater, a consumer of alcohol, and a womanizer), but in the end he always wins out over his patron and his rivals. Moreover, in line with the usual direction of transformation we have noted, even the refined notion of *rasa*, the poetic "flavor" or "mood," is now an actual fluid dripping from the "text."

The *cāṭu* tradition has its own understanding of Kālidāsa's death (indeed, the theme of a poet's death, and the last moment before, recurs throughout this corpus). Kālidāsa had been cursed by his wife to die because of a woman (this because the poet refused to sleep with her, arguing that since she had sent him to become educated, she was really his mother); and the curse worked itself out in the following way. The king offered one half of a *śloka* verse as a riddle and promised a handsome prize to whoever could complete it.

kusume kusumôtpattiḥ śrūyate na ca dṛśyate

Flower growing on flower:
we've heard of this, but never seen it.

At this time Kālidāsa was living with a courtesan, who heard the riddle and at once rushed home to ask the poet how to answer it. Kālidāsa effortlessly completed the verse:

bāle tava mukhâmbhoje katham indīvara-dvayam

How is it, my beauty, that two blue lilies
are planted on the lotus
that is your face?

The greedy courtesan learned this line by heart and then killed her famous lover, carving up his body with a knife and scattering the limbs all over her backyard. She went to the court to claim the prize. The king at once acknowledged the correctness and beauty of her solution, but somehow doubted that this woman had really improvised the line herself; so he sent his soldiers to investigate in the courtesan's house. They found Kālidāsa's severed head, still chanting the answer to the riddle.

Clearly, it is dangerous to answer a riddle. Pat answers are especially suspect—certain, really, to be wrong. The riddle creates its own predictable, neat, and finally deflating response. But what makes this lurid story still more interesting is the implied criticism of the Sanskrit poet's hackneyed, utterly conventionalized metaphors (*ḳavi-samaya*). All women's faces are like the lotus, all eyes dark as the water lily. So overworked are these metaphors that they lose all life, become useless pleonastic excrescences on the body of language. On this level, it is perhaps significant that they cost the poet his life.

A powerful, direct attack on frozen literary convention comes from a well-known Tamil story, appropriated by the Telugu tradition at Kāḷahasti, about the classical poet Nakkīrar—here the president of the Sangam "Academy" that judged and examined poetry in Maturai, in the far south of the Tamil land. This story follows the standard *cāṭu* pattern of lifting a verse from a major text and providing a narrative context for its appearance. In effect, a striking medieval example of the *cāṭu* process has crossed the boundary of the oral *cāṭu* milieu and worked its way into fixed literary texts such as Parañcotimuṉivar's *Tiruviḷaiyāṭaṟ-purāṇam* (in Tamil) and Dhūrjaṭi's *Kāḷahasti-māhātmyamu* (in Telugu).[18] We summarize the story from the medieval Tamil versions (although in some ways it is Dhūrjaṭi's retelling that most clearly reveals its subversive potential). First, however, we cite the verse in question—*Kuṟuntŏkai* 2, an ancient poem ascribed to Iṟaiyaṉār (literally, "the Lord"), ostensibly addressed to a bee:

kŏṅkuter vāḻkkaiy añciṟait tumpi
kāmañ cĕppātu kaṇṭatu mŏḻimo
payiliyatu keḻīiya naṭpiṉ mayiliyaṟ
ceṟiyĕyiṟ ṟarivai kūntaliṉ
naṟiyavum uḷavonīy aṟiyum pūve

You who spend your life in flight,
seeking a hidden sweetness:
don't tell me what I want to hear,
tell me what you really see.
I love a woman, love everything
about her—the way she walks,
just like a peacock; her teeth,
her long dark hair
more fragrant, I think, than any flower—
but only you can say.

Thus the ancient poem as we find it in our texts. How did it come to be composed, and with what consequences? And what is the meaning of the ascription to Iṟaiyaṉār, "the Lord"?

One evening the Pāṇḍya king went for a walk in his garden,

18. See also the chapter "Nakkīraccarukkam" in the version of *Cīkāḷatti-purāṇam* by Tuṟaimaṅkalam Civappirakācacuvāmikaḷ, Karuṇaippirakācacuvāmikaḷ, and Velaiyacuvāmikaḷ (Madras: Memorial Press, 1948).

where he was overwhelmed by sweet fragrances. A thought came into his mind: what, he wondered, was more fragrant—the flowers of his royal garden, or his queen's dark hair? Unable to resolve this difficult question, he hung a bag of gold coins at the entrance to the Academy of Sciences and promised this reward to any poet who could compose a verse expressing the king's secret thought. The poets of the academy all tried their hand at composing such a verse, but none succeeded in divining the king's dilemma.

Now there was, in Maturai, a poor Brahmin, Tarumi, who wanted to get married but could not afford to; so he went into the temple of Lord Śiva-Sundareśvara and said to the god, "You know what goes on in everyone's mind. Please give me a poem that expresses the king's secret thought." Śiva composed the poem that begins *kŏṅkuter vaḻkkaiy añciṟait tumpi* [*Kuṟuntŏkai* 2, see above] and gave it to Tarumi, who at once read it in the academy. When the king heard the poem, he acknowledged that it hit the mark exactly; but as he was about to give the coins to Tarumi, Nakkīrar, the president of the academy, stopped him. "There is a flaw," said Nakkīrar, "in this verse."

In despair, Tarumi rushed back to the temple and said, indignantly, to the god: "Why did you give me a flawed poem?" At this Śiva, very angry, emerged out of the *liṅga* in the form of a poet and, striding into the academy, asked, "Who finds fault with my poem?" "I do," said Nakkīrar. "And what is the flaw?" "It is not," said Nakkīrar, "in the domains of phonology or of morphology; rather, it is a mistake in meaning."[19] "And what is

19. These are the three major divisions of Tamil grammar: *ĕḻuttu* (phonology), *cŏl* (morphology), and *pŏruḷ* (meaning).

that mistake?" demanded Śiva. "Everyone knows," said Nakkīrar, "that no woman has naturally fragrant hair: a woman's hair becomes fragrant only when she adorns it with flowers."

"Is this true of the divine dancing girls in Indra's world?" asked the god, and Nakkīrar insisted that it was. "And what of the goddess whom you yourself worship, the Lady whose Tresses are Fragrant with Wisdom (Jñāna-prasūnâmbikā, at Kāḷahasti)?" asked Śiva. "The same rule applies to her," said Nakkīrar, stubborn and embattled. At this the god opened slightly the third eye in his forehead, which burns whatever it sees, but the president of the academy—true to type—remained firm: "Even were you the god Indra himself, and your whole body full of eyes,[20] a mistake remains a mistake." By now, however, the third eye was fully open, and Nakkīrar had to jump into the Golden Lotus Tank in the Maturai temple to escape being burnt to cinders. He emerged only to sing a poem in praise of Śiva, Lord of Kāḷahasti; and he then had to relearn the basics of the Tamil alphabet from Murukaṉ, the god of Tamil.[21]

The Kāḷahasti tradition extends the story: here Śiva curses Nakkīrar to become a leper and to wander in this repugnant form until he sees Mount Kailāsa, home to the god. The erstwhile scholar-poet wanders north to Kāḷahasti, where a demon imprisons him in a cave with ninety-nine other victims. Now

20. Indra is Sahasrâkṣa, "marked by a thousand eyes."

21. The summary follows Parañcotimuṉivar. For a more complete discussion, see D. Shulman, "From Author to Non-Author in Tamil Literary Legend," *Journal of the Institute of Asian Studies* 10 (1993), 1–23. And see the afterword by V. Narayana Rao in V. Narayana Rao and Hank Heifetz, *For the Lord of the Animals* (Berkeley: University of California Press, 1987).

that Nakkīrar has come, there is a full hundred—enough of a mouthful, at last, for the demon to eat. In this moment of ultimate distress, Nakkīrar prays to Subrahmaṇya, who kills the demon and saves the poet; and since Kāḷahasti is known as the Southern Kailāsa, the poet's sickness is also cured. He sings a poem of a hundred verses to the god at Kāḷahasti and ends with a remarkable prayer:

ī saṃsāramu duḥkhâ-
vāsânandambu dīni varjimpaṃgān
e sukhamu galugu daya nann'
ā sukhamuna gūrpave kṛtārthuḍan agudun

Joy, in life, is never unmixed
with pain. If there is some special comfort
in letting go of the world,
lead me to it now, in love.[22]

The story of Nakkīrar emerges naturally out of the *cāṭu* milieu and reflects its major drives. The crusty old president of the academy, obsessed with conventional rules and forms, cannot even see the beauty of the verse that the god has improvised and that gives voice to the king's uncertainty. Iṟaiyaṉār-Śiva's poem is rich with feeling, resistant to simple classification; Nakkīrar defends the *kavi-samaya*, the laws governing poetic practice, with all the arrogance of the norm-bound, dry-as-dust scholar. The story is thus about his transformation—from desiccated academic to devotional poet who has experienced suffering and sings of it from the heart, as the *cāṭu* literati would demand.

22. Dhūrjaṭi, *Śrīkāḷahasti-māhātmyamu* (Madras: Vāviḷḷa Rāmasvāmiśāstrulu and Sons, 1966), 3.221.

Once again, a classical verse, extracted from its text, serves as the nucleus for a narrative that comments incisively on the structure of the tradition as a whole and exposes its internal strains.

Notions of authority, and the values that underlie it, change over time, and these changes are themselves sometimes recorded in the oral literary lore surrounding the texts. The Nakkīrar story begins with a powerful image of traditional literary authority—the academy in Maturai, which serves as an ultimate judge of a poem's merit. The image is an ancient one in the Tamil sources, first fully attested in the commentary (also ascribed to a Nakkīrar—historically distinct from the Sangam-period poet) on *Iṟaiyaṉār Akappŏruḷ*, an fifth- or sixth-century handbook on the poetic grammar of love. There we hear of three such academies of scholars and poets—the last apparently associated with the corpus we know today as Sangam poetry. The medieval tradition, however, has transformed this august image and concretized it in a manner entirely appropriate to the *cāṭu* vision of things. The Tamil Sangam was seated, so we are told, on a plank—originally just a small board—that floated in the Golden Lotus Tank inside the great temple of Sundareś-vara-Śiva at Maturai. This plank would expand to make room for any suitably gifted poet but would offer no space to an incompetent one. There was, then, an empirical, objective standard for good poetry in Maturai. No room for doubt or confusion: either the plank accepted you or it didn't. By the end of the medieval period, when the *cāṭu* tradition was at its height, a further development in the story took place. Now we are told that the pedantic scholars of the Sangam—securely ensconced on the plank—took exception to the devotional verses of Nammāḻvār, the central figure of Tamil Vaiṣṇava *bhakti* poetry. A single, very simple verse of this great poet was written on a palm leaf and placed on the Sangam plank. At once the plank unceremoniously dumped all the scholars and poets into the water, leaving room only for Nammāḻvār's written verse.[23]

In Telugu, some of the most outrageous *cāṭus* are associated with the name of Tĕnāli Rāmaliṅgaḍu, whom we have met as the clown-jester-poet (*vikaṭa-kavi*) situated by the *cāṭu* narratives in Kṛṣṇadevarāya's court. Like any good *cāṭu* poet, Tĕnāli Rāma improvises verses to stunning effect; but most of these verses include a pointed attack on some rival figure, usually a representative of pompous authority. Some of these *cāṭus* are utterly beyond translation; one of them is not even capable of being graphically reproduced. It reveals a tension, if not outright competition, between the literate tradition of the scholarly court and the oral tradition of the *cāṭu*.

A certain scribe came to the court of Kṛṣṇadevarāya and claimed that he could write anything down as fast as a poet could dictate to him. Tĕnāli Rāma was ready with his tricks. He began reciting a verse which makes perfect sense as an oral utterance, metrically and lexically correct, but full of nonsense sounds commonly used in oral speech. The verse opens with a bilabial continuous fricative, *tṛvvv*, which in common speech indicates nonexistence. There is no way, however, to reproduce this phonetic sequence in Telugu script.

tṛvvv-aṭa bābā talapai
puvv'aṭa jābilli valva būd'aṭa cede
buvvaṭa kalarūpu hḷhḷak-
kavvaṭa velayaṅgan'aṭṭi harunaku jeje

23. *Vinota-raca-mañcari*, 167.

Whoooooooshh—no father.
Moon-flower on head.
Ashes for clothes.
Poison for food.
A body? Fizzzzzzzzzzzzzzzzzzed out.
That's the god for me.

Even though the poem is represented in writing here, in transliteration, it is a poem that has to be spoken.[24] It does have lexical consistency, of a kind: it describes Lord Śiva who has no (*tṛvvv*) father and no visible form. But this residual semanticity is also part of the joke and the jester's peculiar power. The self-confident scribe was, of course, discomfited; the jester, as always, has triumphed by his wit, which is based on a linguistic precision and an awareness that transcend all normal habits of conceptualizing speech.

At times, Tĕnāli Rāma brings his wit to bear against rival poets, as in the case of Mŏlla, a low-caste woman poet who brought her poems to Tĕnāli Rāma and was rewarded with the following parodic verse:

cīpara pāpara tīgala
cepala buṭṭ' allinaṭlu cĕppĕḍu nī ī
k̤āpu k̤avitvapu k̤ūtalu
bapana-k̤avi-varuni cĕvik̤i pramadamb' iḍune

You make poems as if weaving a basket to hold fish
out of any old bamboo strips.

24. Another poem attributed to Tĕnāli Rāma is full of indexical pronouns that can be understood only in association with appropriate gestures in context.

Could any Brahmin put up with
your howlers?

Again we hear a tension between the oral-literary and the high-caste norms—but here, for once, the jester is on the side of authority and status.

A slightly more complicated example, ridiculing poets who look for patrons everywhere, is another poem-by-committee with a punch line by Tĕnāli Rāma.

Four poets—Pĕddana, Bhaṭṭumūrti, Timmana, and Tĕnāli Rāma—went to visit Kṛṣṇadevarāya. On their way into the court they were stopped by the doorman, Timmaḍu, a low-caste washerman. Hoping to please him, so that he would eventually allow them in, the poets composed, together, the following verse:

Pĕddana: *vākiṭi kāvali timma*

O Timma, you guard the doorway.

Bhaṭṭumūrti: *prākaṭamuga sukavivarula pāliṭi sŏmma*

We rise or fall: your hands hold the key.

Timmana: *nīk' idĕ padyamu kŏmma*

Here's a poem just for you. Please take it.

Tĕnāli Rāma: *nāk' ī paccaḍamĕ cālu nayamugan imma*

The shirt off your back is gift enough—for me!

The first three poets shamelessly flatter the doorman in the usual mode, seeking to ingratiate themselves by elevating him to the role of a patron. Tĕnāli Rāma mocks this situation, in which poems are offered only in expectation of expensive gifts—even from a lowly doorman. The clown, naturally, is the only one to claim anything substantial from this interchange.

Cāṭus tend, then, to be subversive, holding arbitrary, arid rules and prior conventions up to scrutiny, always demanding a return to bodily experience and concrete sensation. At times this trend toward the outrageous can produce poems that are obviously obscene, like the following verse attributed to Śrīnātha (another *nindā-stuti*, "praise-through-blame," on Śiva, here in his guise as the god who drank the deadly Hālāhala poison produced from churning the ocean of milk):

k̤āla-k̤andhara īśāna phālanetra
nīdu viṣam' āragiñcina cedu bova
k̤ŏmma meḍūri k̤amma cak̤ora-netra
panasatonavanṭi bhagamu cumbanamu ceyumā

Black-Throat, Śiva, my God:
if you want to get rid of the bitter taste
that poison left in your mouth,
try licking the cunt of that Kamma woman from Meḍūru,
juicy as a slice of summer jackfruit.[25]

5. HISTORY AND COMMUNITY

One of the most impressive achievements of the *cāṭu* milieu is its creation of a powerful narrative context for its remembered

25. Collected by C. P. Brown: see G. Lalita, *Tĕlugulo cāṭu-k̤avitvam* (Vijayawada: Kvāliṭī Publishers, 1981), 47. The final line is metrically incorrect, by classical standards. Viresalingam bowdlerized this verse, replacing *bhagamu* with *talamu*: *Āndhra-k̤avula caritramu* (1917), 534.

verses—nearly always the court of a great king. In the case of Telugu, this king is Kṛṣṇadevarāya, supposedly surrounded by eight famous poets (the *aṣṭa-dig-gajas*). For Sanskrit, we have Bhoja of Dhara, the supposed patron of Kālidāsa and Bhavabhūti. Tamil places its corresponding moment of poetic flowering in the Choḻa court, where Kampaṉ, Ŏṭṭakkūttar, and Pukaḻenti play out their rivalries. In all these cases, we find the image of a poet-king who, like the philosopher-king of the Greek tradition, appealed to the imagination of the literate communities and provided a model for aspiring rulers. Kṛṣṇadevarāya loved to be called *sāhitī-samarâṅgaṇa-sārvabhauma*, a monarch who rules the fields of both poetry and battle. A good king is measured by his appreciation of good poetry and by his generosity to poets. Poets took pride in their ability to make kings famous—or, if they were thwarted by their patrons, to bring down ruin upon them. The arena in which these claims were articulated was that of *cāṭus* and their attached narratives.

To ask about the historicity of these paradigmatic poet-kings and their court poets is entirely to miss the point; as we argued earlier, this is a tradition intent upon creative forms of intertextuality, to be achieved only by bringing different poetic voices together and by exploring their complex resonances. Nonetheless, there is a historical dimension to this tradition, which is linked to the new elite formation of late-medieval south India and to the internal processes of evolution within the regional cultures. The Telugu *cāṭu* tradition, as we know it today, seems to stem primarily from the mid–seventeenth century, which was already looking backward, with nostalgia, to the imperial culture of Vijayanagara of the early sixteenth century (the period of Kṛṣṇadevarāya and Pĕddana). Seventeenth-century Andhra had its own particular forms of creativity and intellectual synthesis; in some senses, current literary legend to the contrary notwithstanding, it is this moment which marks the real culmination of the classical Telugu tradition.

The idealized *cāṭu* universe, with its famous poets and royal patrons, is one of the major expressive frames for this tradition. In this mode, Kṛṣṇadevarāya becomes the magnetic center of a very vibrant world of poets, pandits, critics, courtesans, and one outstanding jester-clown. The latter, Tĕnāli Rāmaliṅgaḍu, in some sense epitomizes the *cāṭu* vision—innovative, subversive, trenchant in judgment, spontaneous, and heavily weighted toward the oral as opposed to the scholarly-literate (as we have seen). Much ink has been wasted in an attempt to show that this beloved figure was identical with the *kāvya* poet called Tĕnāli Rāmakṛṣṇa, again of the sixteenth century. There is, however, no reason whatsoever to believe that the jester Tĕnāli Rāmaliṅgaḍu was a historical person, let alone that the great *kāvya* poet attracted this role to himself. Jesters existed at the Vijayanagara court, as we know from temple iconography at Hampi and elsewhere; but Tĕnāli Rāmaliṅgaḍu belongs, by right, to the moment when the Telugu *cāṭu* system crystallized in a retrospective frame. The system needed just such an outrageous figure; his appearance in the stories is one sure sign that we are dealing not with memory but with a critical imagination working on materials suited to the middle-level elite of late-medieval Andhra.[26]

We can say something about this elite community. It was,

26. For some of these stories, see D. Shulman, *The King and the Clown in South Indian Myth and Poetry* (Princeton: Princeton University Press, 1985), 180–200.

first of all, literate—but not a group of scholars. The verses in circulation suggest that this community was very refined in its taste. It was not, however, located in the royal centers; rather, it belonged to the villages and the smaller towns—*not* the big city. It was an upper-caste and middle-caste community, almost entirely male; the only women that might have participated in it were courtesans, who served men's pleasure. There was significant Brahmin contribution to shaping values and conceptions, and many Brahmin literati were carriers of the entire tradition. But there was also a large role for non-Brahmin, mostly left-hand (nonagriculturalist) castes who came to prominence and political power throughout Andhra and Tamil Nadu as the imperial center at Vijayanagara collapsed. We have elsewhere referred to this new elite by the catch-all term *Nāyaka*, and spoken of its conspicuous values—a new type of individualism and subjectivity, a somewhat ironic heroism, a fascination with the body (indeed with the tangible, sensual, and concrete generally) as the locus of true experience, a dynamism in social attitudes and a cultural investment in more fluid patterns of political and economic formation, a more integrated vision of the self, and so on.[27] These values are frequently evident in the Telugu *cāṭus* and influenced the selection of the most popular verses held in the community's memory.

We should also note that this community within which *cāṭus* circulated and were generated was a multilingual one. Along with Telugu, Sanskrit, and possibly to some extent Tamil and

27. See V. Narayana Rao, D. Shulman, and Sanjay Subrahmanyam, *Symbols of Substance: Court and State in Nāyaka-Period Tamil Nadu* (Delhi: Oxford University Press, 1992).

Kannada, operated within this cultural sphere. Language boundaries were porous, and *cāṭu* verses moved easily from one language to another. Thus we find Sanskrit versions of Telugu and Tamil *cāṭus*, and vice versa. This is a period in which Sanskrit is often borrowing from regional languages. While there are instances and contexts in which Sanskrit serves as an instrument of legitimation and prestige, in the case of the *cāṭu* world, at least, Sanskrit is simply one more possible vehicle for *cāṭu* poetry, not necessarily superior in any sense to the regional languages. Moreover, the Sanskrit of the *cāṭu* verses is often texturally and syntactically close to the regional languages, as if the poets had merely switched register, playfully extending the range of their voices.

The consolidation of this middle-level, educated elite *outside* the royal courts was the necessary condition for the emergence of the integrated, relatively standardized, heavily intertextual *cāṭu* world, and allowed for the kind of generative commentary on the classic works of the Telugu tradition that we have been exploring. It produced the images of the poets and patrons, of scholars and subversive clowns, that we have tried to define, along with the highly specific understanding of poetic language and its powers exemplified in the *cāṭu* verses. It also made possible the systematic integration of these conceptions in the richly textured web of story enveloping the poems. Moreover, this integrated vision is itself linked to other creative developments in seventeenth-century south India, for example, to the surprising emergence of new historiographical modes[28] and to the crystal-

28. As we see in Telugu works such as *Rāyavācakamu*, a retrospective "history" of Kṛṣṇadevarāya's time, and the *Tañjāvūri āndhra rājula caritra*,

lization of medieval Telugu grammatical theory (with the related metaphysics of grammar) that we see in the works of Appakavi and Piṅgali Sūranna.[29] Indeed, both historiography and grammar of these new types are implicitly present in the *cāṭus*. The retrospective elaboration of an imagined *cāṭu* universe, projected backwards into the court of Kṛṣṇadevarāya, is thus part of a much wider intellectual maturation in the Telugu-speaking region as the classical tradition reached toward new heights. This same process was also going on, though with distinct institutional and social features, in the Tamil country to the south—which was, by the seventeenth century, largely ruled by Telugu-speaking kings.

We need to stress that this extended period of crystallization is by no means the origin of the *cāṭu* phenomenon. *Cāṭu* verses, and stories about them, existed in Sanskrit for many centuries and may well be a very ancient feature of all major Indian literary traditions. Regional collections, such as Merutuṅga's *Prabandha-cintāmaṇi* from the northwest of the subcontinent, exist and reflect the particular cultural configurations which produced them. Nonetheless, there seems to be a specifically Deccan substratum to the *cāṭu* system that we know in south India. The most popular collection of Sanskrit *cāṭu* traditions—

---

to name only two. We are preparing a study, together with Sanjay Subrahmanyam, of the range of historiographical thought in late-medieval south India. And see Phillip Wagoner, *Tidings of the King: A Translation and Ethnohistorical Analysis of the Rāyavācakamu* (Honolulu: University of Hawaii Press, 1993).

29. Appakavi offers an eloquent myth about the origin of grammar; Sūranna has produced a masterpiece of linguistic metaphysics, the *Kaḷāpūrṇodayamu*, which we hope to describe in another monograph.

the so-called *Bhoja-prabandha*, which contains many of the stories we have cited[30]—seems oriented toward Ekaśilānagara, that is, the Kākatīya capital Orugallu/Warrangal in the northeastern Deccan. Thus Kālidāsa takes himself to Ekaśilānagara at Bhoja's death. Here again, this vision of Warrangal is almost certainly retrospective, a projection backward toward a necessary and creatively remembered past. It is, however, not unlikely that the same cultural milieu that produced this work remained active in the Deccan groups that ultimately founded the Nāyaka successor-states to the imperial center and in the literary worlds they constructed.

The *cāṭu* system radiated outward and was, it seems, related to similar creations in other regions. In the Tamil country the Choḻa court served as the focus for stories about the major poets—and it is worth noting, in passing, that the process of selection excluded many prominent figures, such as Cayaṅkŏṇṭār and Cekkiḻār: not every classical work finds its way into the tradition. Again, these stories clearly evolved and became systematized only much later, probably in Nāyaka times. The first serious attempt to produce a cohesive collection of narrativized verses, the *Tamiḻ nāvalar caritai*, may be as late as the eighteenth century; and, as is elsewhere the case, this very attempt at anthologization and ordering reflects an attenuation of the living oral transmission and the emergence of another stage. It is also fascinating to observe an analogous efflorescence of *cāṭu*-like stories in the milieu of Persian poetry cultivated at the Mughal court. Here, too, we have stories drawn from—or, perhaps more

30. The very existence of this text in Sanskrit, entirely devoted to *cāṭus*, is itself remarkable evidence of elite recognition of the *cāṭu* tradition.

precisely, projected backward into—the more distant past. Thus the sultan of Bengal, Ghiyāth al-Dīn, sets up a poetry contest around a personal incident in his life, which the poets have to guess; the contest is resolved only when a famous ghazal (*Sāqi, hadith-i sarv . . .*) is sent to the sultan's court by the great Ḥāfiz himself, from distant Iran.[31] Ḥāfiz, like the south Indian *cāṭu* poet, has natural omniscience expressed in precise and perfectly controlled language. There is a clustering of such stories from the seventeenth and eighteenth centuries in the north, just as the Telugu *cāṭu* system was entering into its formative phase in Andhra.[32]

6. *CĀṬU* TRADITION IN THE TWENTIETH CENTURY

The tradition remained a living one well into modern times in south India, and many stories, personally attested, reveal the way it worked, generating new verses and molding older ones to its purposes. The printing press also added a new dimension to the spread of *cāṭus*. Many *muktaka* verses composed by individual poets and published in literary magazines quickly entered into oral circulation, becoming *cāṭus* in the process. New legends about contemporary poets circulated among the literati, and *cāṭus* grew around them. The early decades of the twentieth century witnessed a profound renewal of oral versification, led

31. We wish to thank Muzaffar Alam for discussing this ghazal with us.

32. Similar stories exist, of course, for the poets of the Delhi Sultanate—just as the Sanskrit *cāṭu* tradition antedates the systemic movement of late-medieval Andhra. The same obsession with historicity that has characterized attitudes toward the Telugu *cāṭus* applies, mutatis mutandis, to the north Indian stories about great poets.

by Divākarla Tirupati Śāstri (1872–1920) and Cĕllapilla Veṅkaṭa Śāstri (1870–1950). These two poets, popularly known together as Tirupati-Veṅkaṭa-Kavulu, "the Tirupati-Veṅkaṭa poets," or *janṭa-kavulu*, "Twin Poets," performed phenomenal feats of oral improvisation and memory all over Andhra. Their specialty was *śatâvadhāna*: dozens of "questioners," *pṛcchakas*, up to a hundred, would announce their names and give the poets problem questions, puzzles, or a riddle-line meant to become part of a verse; the poets would have to improvise correct answers, in verse, in the order in which they were asked, one line at time, thus producing a *muktaka* verse for each questioner. At the end of the performance, the poets had to recite again, in the proper order, all the (hundred or so) verses they had composed. Their performances, rich with fun, scholarly skill, and wit, energized the literary community and produced a veritable beehive of oral verses. On street corners, in restaurants, clubs, and at gatherings of friends, people would recite the latest verses of Tirupati-Veṅkaṭa-Kavulu.

We can take a few short examples by way of illustrating this process of producing new *cāṭus*. One day the poets were given the following puzzling line as a *samasyā* riddle:

mā kuladāsay ĕntay abhimānamu ledura candraśekharā

literally: "Candraśekhara, slave of our family, you have no shame"

Here is the poem they improvised around this final line:

nāku vibūdi-rāyaḍ'oka nāyakuḍāy ani nīdu bhārya rat-
nâkaru cĕṭṭa baṭṭinadiy ārasiy unḍiyu sigguleka nīv'
ākuḷatan grahiñciyunun audala dālcitiv'aura bhā-
mā-kula-dāsay ĕntay abhimānamu ledura candraśekharā

The penultimate line now ends with *bhā-*, which attaches to the first part of the final line to give the sense: "a slave to women" (*bhāmā-kula-dāsa*).

The poem builds on the myth that Śiva carries the river Ganges on his head and loves her more than his other wife, Pārvatī. The Ganges also flows into the ocean (*ratnâkara*), seen as a storehouse of gems and other precious stones. It is well known that Śiva wears ashes all over his body and has to beg for a living. We now get a slightly impertinent portrait of this god:

> You own nothing but worthless ashes,
> so your fickle wife rejects you
> and takes a rich and fluent lover.
> Though you know all about it, Śiva,
> still you carry her on your head.
>
> Candraśekhara, Moon-crested god:
> you must be hooked
> on women.

But this is only the first part of the process. The *cāṭu* milieu needs a story and easily made one up around this verse. There must be a man named Candraśekhara (Moon-crested = Śiva) in town. His wife has an affair with a rich local merchant (*ratnâkara*, an "ocean of jewels"). Chandraśekhara knows about the affair and meekly accepts it, remaining married to his wife, whom he still loves. People in the city, however, regard him as spineless. The poets bring this scandal indirectly into the open with a punning verse ostensibly about Śiva, but subtly referring to the cuckolded husband under cover of the *samasyā*. The story now illuminates and reframes the verse, which also elevates and enlivens the story in the classic feedback loop of the *cāṭu* process.

Being peripatetic, these two poets were said to have women in every town—in accordance with the romantic image of the *cāṭu* poet, as we have seen with reference to Kālidāsa, Kampaṉ, Śrīnātha, and Dhūrjaṭi. The paradigm persists right into the modern age. (In "reality," these two poets led very disciplined and traditional lives.) There are, of course, *cāṭus* meant to substantiate this favored image. Here is a verse said to have been composed by Veṅkaṭa Śāstri for his friend Tirupati Śāstri when the latter urged him to hit the road one night.

nann' ŏka nāti repaṭi dinambuna poduvu leray añcu vāl-
gannula nīru nimpi tamakamunna gadgada-kaṇṭhiy āyen āy-
annula minna nenu valad'annanu tā vinad' emi setu nan-
mannana cūḍu repaṭi dinammuna podamu lera tirpatī

A certain lady has said to me, "Don't go today. You can leave
tomorrow." She had tears in her eyes, and her voice
was choked. If I tell her "No," she doesn't listen.
What can I do? Try to understand, Tirupati, my friend:
Give me one more day.

The senior partner of the two poets, Veṅkaṭa Śāstri, was revered as guru by a number of young poets of the time, who later grew famous in their own right. Following the trend set by Tirupati-Veṅkaṭa-Kavulu, some of these younger poets teamed up with a friend and wrote as a pair. Among them were the two poets Kāṭūri Veṅkaṭeśvara Rāvu and Piṅgali Lakṣmīkāntam (the latter was the first Professor of Telugu at Andhra University in Waltair). They dedicated a book of theirs—*Saundaranandamu*, a Telugu version of Aśvaghoṣa's Sanskrit classic—to Veṅkaṭa Śāstri, who, in a public ceremony, gave his blessings in verse to his disciples. These verses were later published as an appendix to the book. In one line Veṅkaṭa Śāstri addresses his twin disciples as a single person, combining their names into one compound:

Lakṣmīkāntâhvaya-veṅkaṭeśvara-kavī

Poet Veṅkaṭeśvara, named Lakṣmīkānta

Now it was widely believed that Veṅkaṭeśvara Rāvu was the one with real poetic skills, while Lakṣmīkāntam merely lent the pair his name. So the innocent phrase used by Veṅkaṭa Śāstri came to acquire a suggestive quality when the line was quoted publicly: the real poet (*kavi*) was Veṅkaṭeśvara, while Lakṣmīkāntam was only a name (*āhvaya*). Here is the *cāṭu* system at work, lifting a line of poetry, breaking it irregularly in the middle, and using it to comment upon and rank two well-known poets.

As in medieval times, so in the twentieth century masters of oral improvisation competed as rivals. Another set of Twin Poets—known as Rāma-Kṛṣṇa-Kavulu, i.e., Oleṭi Veṅkaṭa-rāma-śāstri and Vedula Rāma-kṛṣṇa-śāstri—were contemptuously called *jīlugu-bĕṇḍlu*, "corkstops," by the Tirupati-Veṅkaṭa-Kavulu. The implication was that these long-standing rivals, with whom the Tirupati-Veṅkaṭa-Kavulu carried on a contentious and lively argument in verse, were light-weight poets. The Rāma-Kṛṣṇa-Kavulu, however, happily accepted, and twisted, the humiliating image in a newly improvised verse hurled back at their rivals, who are now identified by an even more insulting metaphor:

kā-kavi-kāca-pātrala mŏgambulu mūyaga jīlgu-bĕṇḍlame

Yes, we are proud to be corks
to seal the mouths of glass bottles
filled with tasteless poems.

Not to be outdone, Tirupati-Veṅkaṭa-Kavulu then escalated the clash of metaphors:

kākavi! kāca-pātrala mŏgambulu mūsĕḍu jīlgu-bĕṇḍlakum
jekurune sabhā-sthitiyu jekurekāk' adi tad-rasambulan
gai kŏnuvelan ŏkka kaḍagā baḍavaivarĕ paṭṭupaṭṭinan
meku bigiñci lāgi balimin balu mukkalu seyakundure

You tasteless poets! Are corks that seal glass bottles
honored in the royal court? And even if they were,
when you drink from the bottle, you throw the cork away.
And if it is too tightly in, you twist a corkscrew into it
and pull it out.[33]

This caustic give-and-take in the public medium of poetry remains perfectly within the paradigm of earlier *cāṭus* connected to Tĕnāli Rāmaliṅgaḍu (see, for example, the jester's response to the pandit who claims Telugu poetry is an iron ornament, page 62).

The Tirupati-Veṅkaṭa-Kavulu still belonged entirely to the organic *cāṭu* world, continuous with the medieval past. Patterns of patronage, composition, and circulation were essentially no different from those in Śrīnātha's time—even though the poets now traveled by train, and their verses came to be printed. But these great oral poets also mark the last efflorescence of the me-

33. Tirupati-Veṅkaṭa-Kavulu, *Gīratamu* (Kadiyam: published by Veṅkaṭa Śāstri's son, 1954), 8–9.

dieval patterns of Telugu poetry. Indeed, one could see their amazing popularity and success as in some way constituting a reaction to the encroachment of modern printing upon the domain of popular communication.[34] Printing was the object of great fascination and welcomed as an opportunity to render literary works "permanent," but it may also have been unconsciously felt as a threat to the world of oral improvisation—although at first printed editions were little more than functional substitutes for palm-leaf manuscripts, and did not actually replace the received (orally transmitted) texts or change the manner of their use.[35] But from this point on, the perceived threat gradually became real, and the entire literary world was transformed.

With respect to *cāṭus* and the cultural milieu that nourished them, the printing press eventually instigated very major changes. For one thing, print changed the concept of factuality. The privileged status printing acquired over the oral word as a means of communication vastly narrowed the cultural horizon by collapsing the imagination of reality (*pratyakṣī-karaṇa*) and the observation of reality (*pratyakṣa*) into one: imagination was now subjected to constant rupture from a newly privileged, and impoverished, factuality communicated through print. A new *cāṭu* composed within this encompassing frame is now the actual text written by the poet to whom it is attributed; the older mode of displacement by identification, discussed above, has given way to a form of authorship in which the poet is made to

34. This argument has been presented more elaborately in V. Narayana Rao, *Tĕlugulo kavitā-viplavāla svarūpam*, 107–11.

35. For the distinction between received and recorded texts, see the introduction.

coincide with himself, individually and biographically conceived, instead of the poem's coinciding with a self-consciously retrojected image or style. The new *cāṭu* may still be orally circulated, but it is more often published in journals or newspapers. With the repeated interference of a printed text, improvisations and textual variations practically disappear. Even legends related to the *cāṭus* are now, strange to say, verified for their actual occurrence. The text of a *cāṭu* can be closely checked with the author for its authenticity. In the new environment there is little room for communal creation of *cāṭus*; instead the community is reduced to the role of their consumer.

Meanwhile, the *cāṭu* community itself was fast changing its form. It was no longer the village elite gathered under the banyan tree. Rather, we are dealing with a graphically literate middle class, distributed over cities and towns and given to reading newspapers or, later, to watching TV. People of this class do not sing verses; such recitation has gone out of fashion. They merely listen to verses. Furthermore, the printing press eventually rendered both verse and meter obsolete. The primary mode of poetry for most readers—who read silently in the privacy of their homes—has become the nonmetrical prose poem (*vacana-kavitvam*). A silent world of individual readers, rather than communal listeners, is not hospitable to the *cāṭu*.[36]

36. Lest this sound like a lament, we would like to note the recent resurgence, within the last five years, of active oral versification in Andhra and Telugu-speaking communities abroad—though not of the *cāṭu* type. *Śatâvadhānis*, or even *sahasrâvadhānis*, who compose verses extempore in answer to the demands of a hundred or a thousand *pṛcchakas*, have become popular on television and in public performance in the cities. Noteworthy among them are Medasani Mohan and Madugula Nagapani Sarma. A

Yet *cāṭus* went on being created, circulated, and remembered, even under these modern conditions. We may mention, by way of illustration and in conclusion, one such modern maker of *cāṭus*—Abbūri Rāmakrishnarao, whose verses were widely circulated in the 1950s. Rāmakrishnarao worked as librarian of Andhra University. One day the principal of the Arts College, Professor Mahadevan, a geologist, called for a meeting with the vice-chancellor to discuss the library's budget. Rāmakrishnarao was uncertain about the place scheduled for the meeting, so he went first to the college, then to the Geology Department office, and finally to the vice-chancellor's residence, to see if Professor Mahadevan was there. Failing to find him anywhere, Rāmakrishnarao sang the following verse, punning both on Mahadevan's geological interests and on his name, that of lord Śiva (and perhaps also gently teasing him for his Tamil origins, insofar as his name becomes transformed into a Sanskrit-Telugu vocative):

bhūmi mīda levu bhūgarbhamuna levu
miṇṭa levu vī si iṇṭa levu
caccipoyināvŏ śambho mahādeva
eṭak̥u povu rāmakṛṣṇa rāvu

You are nowhere above ground,
nor down below in the deeper strata.
You're not in the V.C.'s house,
and you're not in the sky.
Mahādeva, my lord, did you go and die?
If so, where can Rāmakṛṣṇa go?

---

somewhat nostalgic vogue in *cāṭus* is also noticeable on the internet among Telugu speakers.

Another of Rāmakrishnarao's *cāṭus* refers to the well-known fact that the child Kṛṣṇa enjoyed eating dirt—to his mother's horror:[37]

mann'ĕnduku tinnāv' ani
kannayyanu kanna talliy aḍugan andu viṭā-
minnulu kalav' aniy annāḍ' aṭa
vinnāvā muḷḷapūḍi vĕṅkaṭa-ramaṇā

When Kṛṣṇa's mother asked him in anger,
"Why are you eating mud?"
he knew the perfect answer: "Because
it's rich in vitamins!"

In the mid–twentieth century, the *cāṭu* world was still vital and flexible enough to incorporate new medical fads into a classical myth, ironically and lovingly remembered in an orally improvised poem.

37. For a full version of this story, see Wendy Doniger [O'Flaherty], *Hindu Myths* (Harmondsworth: Penguin Books, 1975).

Note on Sources

The most reliable sources for *cāṭu* verses, as defined for this volume, are individuals who memorized the verses as part of their cultural education and used them in community life. A list of written (published) sources for living *cāṭus* is something of a contradiction in terms. Nonetheless, it is sometimes useful or necessary to check recorded sources for other versions of orally collected *cāṭus*, or to complete a verse the person you are collecting from remembers only partially.

There is, however, no good premodern anthology of *cāṭus* (defined as remembered verses), except, perhaps, the Sanskrit *Bhoja-prabandha* and the *Prabandha-cintāmaṇi* of Merutuṅga. Many anthologies of interesting single verses do exist. Some of these verses could be *cāṭus*, but many are either taken from longer narrative poems (*prabandha*) or composed as independent verses (*muktaka*) or clusters of such independent verses (*śatakas* and other genres). The first such collection in Telugu, from about 1420, is Maḍiki Siṅganna's *Sakala-nīti-sammatamu*. Two other anthologies are *Udāharaṇa Padyamulu*, by an anonymous compiler, and *Prabandha-ratnâkaramu*, by Pĕdapāṭi Jagannāthakavi. The two anthologies were included in *Prabandha Ratnāvaḷi*, ed. Veṭūri Prabhākara Śāstri (1918; 2d ed., Hyderabad: Śrī Prabhākara Pariśodhaka Maṇḍali, 1976). Another premodern anthology is *Prabandha-maṇi-bhūṣaṇamu*, an unpublished anthology of an unknown compiler which includes verses by poets who lived before 1750.

Another source of *cāṭus* are texts on meter, where the authors included *cāṭu* verses as illustrations of one metrical feature or another. Among them are Liṅgamaguṇṭa Timmakavi, *Sulakṣaṇa-sāramu* (circa 1550); Kākunūri Appakavi, *Appakavīyamu* (1565); Gaṇapavarapu Veṅkaṭakavi, *Āndhra-prayoga-ratnâkaramu* (circa 1670); Kastūri Raṅgakavi, *Ānanda-raṅgarāṭ-chandamu* (circa 1740); and Kūcimañci Timmakvai, *Sarva-lakṣaṇa-sāra-saṅgrahamu* (circa 1740).

A substantial collection of *cāṭus* was made by C. P. Brown, whose *cāṭu* manuscripts are located in the Oriental Manuscript Library at Madras: D 2884, D 1404, D 12011, and D 13063. Brown collected everything he found, including many verses from people who remembered them orally. The Brown collection, however, remains largely unexplored. Mothī Jagannātha Mal compiled *Śṛṅgāra-padya-ratnâvali* (1903) and *Śṛṅgāra-padya-ratna-śeṣamu* (1911), both of which are *cāṭu* collections. Kandukūri Bālasūryaprasāda Rāyuḍu published a booklet of thirty-three *cāṭu* verses, with a glossary and commentary, under the title *Cāṭu-dhārā-padyamulu* (1903). Vaṅkāyala Kṛṣṇasvāmi Sĕṭṭi collected the erotic verses attributed to Śrīnātha and some anonymous riddling verses and published them as *Vīthi-nāṭak-*

amu, from his own printing press, Śrīraṅgavilāsa Mudrākṣaraśāla (1904; reprint, Madras: 1908). Śrīnātha's erotic verses from this booklet were cleaned of obscenities and reprinted by Vāviḷḷa Rāmasvāmiśāstrulu under the same title, *Vīthi-nāṭakamu*, in 1924. Poems which include riddles and amusements were also covered under *cāṭu* by Kuccerlapāṭi Sūryanārāyaṇa Rāju, who published a volume entitled *Nānârtha-gāmbhīrya-camatkārikā* (Tuni, East Godavari District: Sītārāma-nilaya mudrākṣaraśāla—a printing press owned by the zamindar of Tuni, Raja Vatsavāyi Veṅkaṭa Siṃhâdri Jagapathi Rāju—1892). Perhaps the most noted collection of *cāṭus* is by the great scholar Veṭūri Prabhākara Śāstri, who published two volumes of *Cāṭu-padya-maṇi-mañjari* (vol. I, 1914; rev. ed., 1917: vol. II, 1922; expanded, and part 1 republished in 1952). Dīpāla Piccayya Śāstri's *Cāṭu-padya-ratnâkaramu* (1917) is another important work of *cāṭus*.

A number of verses from extempore poetic performances, *avadhānas*, by scholar-poets have become popular as *cāṭus*. There are several collections of complete *avadhāna* performances, and many more which include only literary riddles, *samasyās*, a standard feature of such performances. See, for example, *Tĕlugu Samasyalu* (Madras: Vyavahāra-taraṅgiṇi Mudrākṣaraśāla, 1880) and *Tĕlugu samasyalu* (Madras: Vāviḷḷa Rāmasvāmiśāstrulu, 1921). Divākarla Tirupati Śāstri and Cĕllapilla Veṅkaṭa Śāstri (the Tirupati-Veṅkaṭa-Kavulu) published several volumes of their oral verse: *Śatâvadhāna-sāramu* (1934), *Nānā-rāja-saṃdarśanamu* (1951; 2d ed., 1967), *Jayanti* (1937), *Jātakacarya* (1934), and *Gīratamu* (1954).

Many *cāṭu* verses related to Telugu poets and their legendary biographies are cited in recent works on the lives of Telugu poets. The first published narrative of the lives of the poets, based on the *cāṭu* legends, is Gurajāḍa Śrīrāmamūrti, *Kavi-jīvitamulu* (printed in fascicles from 1876 on). This work, although stimulated by Macaulay's *Critical and Biographical Essays*, in fact offers the richest available version of the oral materials on the poets, including a collection of five dense *cāṭu* verses called *pañca-pāṣāṇamulu*, "five hard rocks," with glossary. (According to G. Lalita, this glossary is reproduced from a small palm-leaf manuscript, *Camatkāra-cāṭu-padyamulu*, located in Āndhra Sāhitya Pariṣattu, Kākināḍa.)

Important among other works on Telugu poets and incorporating many stories related to the *cāṭus* are Kandukuri Viresalingam, *Āndhra-kavula caritramu*, 3 vols. (Rajahmundry, 1917); Cāgaṇṭi Śeṣayya, *Āndhra-kavi-taraṅgiṇi*, 14 vols. (Kapilesvarapuram, Hindu Dharma Sastra Grantha Nilayamu, 1961); and Arudra, *Samagra-āndhra-sāhityam* (2d rev. ed., Vijayawada: Prajasakti Book House, 1990).

Studies of the *cāṭu* also contain a large number of *cāṭu* verses. Among such works, two stand out: G. Lalita, *Tĕlugulo cāṭu-kavitvam* (Vijayawada: Kvāliṭī Publishers, 1981) and Bŏmmakaṇṭi Śrīnivāsâcāryulu and Bālantrapu Nalinīkāntarāvu, *Tĕlugu cāṭuvu: puṭṭu-pūrvôttarālu* (Madras: Kaḷyāṇi Pracuraṇalu, 1983). The first includes a very interesting selection of *cāṭus* and brief biographical information on many *cāṭu* poets. A healthy feature of this book is that it records the obscene *cāṭus* without substituting dotted lines—a standard practice in post-nineteenth-century publications. The study by Śrīnivāsâcāryulu and Nalinīkāntarāvu is the best we have for Telugu *cāṭus*. In addition to its scholarly excellence and interpretive power, the book also serves as an excellent anthology of a very large number of *cāṭus*, together with an informed commentary and insightful appreciation. An additional feature of this truly remarkable book is that it is virtually free of printing errors. A small pamphlet by Ketavarapu Rāmakoṭi Śāstri, *Āśukavitalu, Avadhānamulu, Cāṭuvlu* (Hyderabad: Andhra Pradesh Sahitya Akademi, 1975) is also to be mentioned in this context for a quick survey of some of the main features of *cāṭus*.

The popularity of *cāṭu* collections has prompted some modern poets to compose independent verses and publish them in literary journals and even as separate books. Verses of political satire by Duggirāla Gopālakṛṣṇayya (1890–1931) became quite popular during the freedom movement. Some of them are collected in *Āndhra-ratna gopāla-kṛṣṇuni cāṭuvulu* (Bejawada: Āndhra-vidyāgoṣṭhi, 1934). Among prominent modern poets whose verses achieved currency as *cāṭus* are Viswanatha Satyanarayana (1895–1976), Abburi Ramakrishna Rao (1896–1979), Devulapalli Krishna Śāstri (1897–1980), and Jalasūtram Rukmiṇīnātha Śāstri (1914–68).

Among Sanskrit collections, in addition to the *Bhoja-prabandha* and *Prabandha-cintāmaṇi* already mentioned, Gaṅgādhara Kṛṣṇa Drāviḍa, *Samayôcita-padya-mālikā* (Bombay: Nirnayasagar Press, 1941) and Allamarāju Subrahmaṇyakavi (1831–92), *Cāṭu-dhārā-camatkāra-sāra*, are of interest.

All Tamil collections of single stanzas, *taṉippāṭal*, confuse the two kinds of *cāṭu* and mostly offer *muktaka* verses. There was enormous productivity in the genre of *muktaka-taṉippāṭal* in Tamil, and many thousands of such verses have survived. Modern anthologies, such as the many-volume series *Taṉippāṭal tiraṭṭu*, edited by Karuppakkiḷar Cu. A. Irāmacāmippulavar and published by the South Indian Saiva Siddhanta Works Publishing Society (1972), are largely taken up with verses of this type, although the late-medieval *cāṭu* tradition, in our sense, is also represented. A more substantial collection of Tamil *cāṭus* associated with *cāṭu* narratives is the *Tamiḻ nāvalar caritai*, perhaps from the eighteenth century, which also marks the first real attempt to record and rationalize, so to speak, this tradition (it offers 270 verses). A much-expanded effort in this direction is Vīracāmi Cĕṭṭiyār's lengthy prose narration of stories about the Tamil (and other) poets, together with many *cāṭus*: *Vinota-raca-mañcari* (Madras, 1867). Still further expansion, and a certain apologetic refashioning, can be found in recent works on individual poets by Puliyūrk Kecikaṉ: *Kampaṉ taṉippāṭalkaḷ*, *Auvaiyār taṉippāṭalkaḷ*, and *Kāḷamekappulavar taṉippāṭalkaḷ*.

A major nineteenth-century compilation is the *Taṉippāṭal tiraṭṭu* by Tillaiyampūrc Cantiracekak-kavirāca-paṇṭitar (though the driving force behind the collection was Pŏṉṉucāmittevar, a minister in the Ramnad court). This collection of 1,248 stanzas, first published by Kalāvati Accakam in 1862, was also reprinted many times, sometimes with helpful commentary. The great pandit M. Raghava Aiyangar printed the first short volume of a *taṉippāṭal* collection in 1935–36: *Pĕrun-tŏkai* (reprint, 1969). Mention should also be made of Mu. Ra. Kantacāmikkavirāyar, *Taṉic-cĕyyuṭ-cintāmaṇi* (1909, 3,815 verses). Perhaps the best modern edition of Tamil *cāṭus* (with the inevitable admixture of *muktaka* and *prabandha* verses) is *Taṉippāṭar-ṟiraṭṭu*, edited by M. Vīraveṟ Piḷḷai (Madras: P. Na. Citampara Mutaliyār Brothers, 1940). For a complete bibliographic survey of *taṉippāṭal* anthologies, see K. V. Zvelebil, *Tamil Literature* (Wiesbaden: Otto Harrassowitz, 1974), 7, 51–54; and there is a serious study of these works—oriented, however, more to the *muktaka* type of *taṉippāṭal*, and blurring the basic typological divide—by Na.

Cekatīcaṉ (Tamiḻaṉpaṉ), *Taṉippāṭal tiraṭṭu: Or Āyvu* (Madras: Paplo Parati Patippakam, 1987).

We have, in general, preferred as texts for this volume *cāṭus* gleaned from living memory: unless otherwise stated, the verses are cited as heard orally. Several people who recalled poems for us are acknowledged in the text. The majority of the Telugu *cāṭus* collected here were remembered by V. Narayana Rao, who heard them as a young man in Andhra. We have, however, always checked these verses with their forms in printed collections, to the extent they were recorded there. The most dependable and comprehensive volume was Bŏmmakaṇṭi Śrīnivāsâcāryulu and Bālantrapu Nalinīkāntarāvu, *Tĕlugu cāṭuvu: puṭṭu-pūrvôttarālu* (1983). In the case of conflict between remembered and printed versions of a given verse, we nearly always chose the remembered one.

Index of First Lines

A heap of dust, lusterless and pale, 78 (Telugu)
A poem made out of Telugu 62 (Sanskrit)
A rich god like Kṛṣṇa can marry 114 (Telugu)
All of Mayilai, great Tiruvāli's home, 101 (Tamil)
At first, we were two, 102 (Tamil)
Bhoja's brilliant fame keeps spreading. 81 (Sanskrit)
Bound by the fantasy of fusing 100 (Tamil)
Break a pot. 119 (Sanskrit)
Condemn me, O Creator, 29 (Sanskrit)
Day by day, we're getting old. 109 (Sanskrit)
Dear X, 95 (Telugu)
Don't eat while you're walking, or laugh while you're talking. 105 (Sanskrit)
Final freedom is that state of no pain, 108 (Sanskrit)
First I killed the king. 31 (Telugu)
Five, four, three, 48 (amil)
Five, six, seven, 79 (Telugu)
Full red lips, breasts, curls, 60 (Telugu)
Full round breasts, body tender as a bud, 72 (Telugu)
Go to hell, damned Creator, 71 (Telugu)
He used to sew leaves together in Gutti 54 (Telugu)
Held-not-held 76 (Tamil)
Her face is like the moon. 90 (Sanskrit)
I can make poems. 49 (Sanskrit)

I know what you're after: 43 (Sanskrit)
I sang of learning, and there was nothing. 74 (Tamil)
I was born for poetry. 133 (Telugu)
I'm Vijjikā, 46 (Sanskrit)
If it happens, it happens. 126 (Tamil)
In agony, the *campaka* blossom wondered 129 (Telugu)
In broad daylight, she's scared of a crow. 82 (Sanskrit)
In Sītā's hands, perfect as the red lotus, 45 (Sanskrit)
In the old days, if a text was demanding, 50 (Telugu)
"Is he a good lover?" 104 (Telugu)
Is poetry a surface sheen, 34 (Telugu)
It was the very first night, 30 (Telugu)
Kālidāsa's poems, 65 (Sanskrit)
King Vīrā-rĕḍḍi has merged into God. 58 (Telugu)
Kumbhakarṇa loved Sleep. 38 (Sanskrit)
Let the Love God aim his arrows 80 (Telugu)
Mornings are for churning oceans. 57 (Tamil)
Music and poetry: 61 (Sanskrit)
My eyes look away in shame. 97 (Tamil)
No ornaments adorn 85 (Sanskrit)
Not entirely hidden, 33 (Telugu)
Not even God can save the money 123 (Telugu)
Now is the time. 107 (Tamil)
One: travel to an alien land. 125 (Telugu)
People with no taste for good poetry 128 (Telugu)
Pressured by the hips from below 66 (Telugu)
She comes down sickened 93 (Telugu)
"Should a monk be eating meat?" 52 (Sanskrit)
Śiva sleeps on Mount Kailāsa. 112 (Telugu)
Speak of courage? Who has courage 98 (Tamil)
Stronger, even, than the bond 132 (Telugu)
That whiff of jasmine, that's my daughter 91 (Telugu)
The beauties of a poem are best known 115 (Telugu)
The bee is drawn to all the blossoms 130 (Sanskrit)
The boss is coming for dinner. 111 (Telugu)
The monkey on the temple wall, 75 (Telugu)
The Moon rests his head in the lap of the Western sky. 55 (Sanskrit)
The Tree of Life is bitter, 127 (Sanskrit)
The village elders gather on the porch of the Rāma temple 40 (Telugu)
The world is really two, made of name and form. 103 (Sanskrit)
There's as much bread as there is dough, 117 (Telugu)
They now read proofs at printing shops 47 (Telugu)

They say a woman has five knots. 32 (Telugu)
They say you saved an elephant— 89 (Telugu)
They taught me "it" was neuter, 68 (Sanskrit)
They're penetrating and profound 84 (Telugu)
Torture us, please, 51 (Telugu)
Total knowledge belongs to God. 41 (Telugu)
Viṣṇu, fortunately, can afford silk. 113 (Telugu)
We knew it's wrong to grow a mustache, 63 (Telugu)
What woman would dare 88 (Telugu)
"What's that thing under your arm?" 53 (Sanskrit)
When a camel gets married, 39 (Sanskrit)
When he would see me on the street, he would halt his elephant 69 (Telugu)
Whispering wonderful whatevers 120 (Sanskrit)
"Who are you, Red-Face, Red-Feet?" 42 (Telugu)
Who needs a basketful of glittering stones? 122 (Telugu)
"Why are you staring at the floor, young lady? 106 (Sanskrit)
Words make the gods give an answer. 116 (Telugu)
Yesterday I saw that lovely woman 94 (Telugu)
You know why the ring finger has no name in Sanskrit? 110 (Sanskrit)
You'll spend thousands in gold on this splendid sari, 73 (Tamil)
You're a drop of water on a lotus leaf. 118 (Telugu)
You're so drunk on wealth and power 37 (Sanskrit)
"You're the best of all my lovers, which is why 96 (Telugu)

Composition: G & S Typesetters, Inc.
Text: 11/15 Granjon
Display: Granjon

www.ingramcontent.com/pod-product-compliance
Lightning Source LLC
Chambersburg PA
CBHW021706230426
43668CB00008B/740